I have used the Who Took My Chalk?™ [*model*] *program at two schools where I have been Principal. The program not only had a positive approach, it was the most interactive and school culturally focused staff development I have ever been involved in. It helped the staff zero in on the issues and provided a non-threatening approach to address those identified issues. Each school did move forward and grow from the experience.*

—Karen Collins, Elementary Principal

All schools today face change, whether led by local initiatives or motivated by external pressures, but few understand the process of change itself. [The] Who Took My Chalk?™ [*model*] *offers clear, practical, down-to-earth advice on how to productively prepare for positive change so that schools can better serve students, and be more rewarding places to work for the adults who serve them.*

—Susan Saltrick, Education Consultant

There are many models that have been proposed for improving student performance in low-performing schools. However, few models begin with the critical steps of building the sense of urgency, trust, support, and consensus among staff within the school in need of improvement. [The] Who Took My Chalk?™ [*model*] *is an impressive tool to do just that. And when school staff are brought together to a shared vision, incredible results will follow.*

—Steve Paine, Retired State Superintendent

[The] Who Took My Chalk?™ [*model*] *gradually transformed our school of highly qualified, veteran teachers into new-age digital facilitators. WTMC provided the answers to our essential question: why, as teachers, do we need to incorporate technology and adapt to new ways of instruction? Throughout the year, WTMC became the reference point in our push of technology integration across the curriculum. Now, teachers are anxious and unafraid to try new technology applications in their classrooms. Our teachers and students are using more technology than ever before, and they are asking "what's next"? When teachers are excited about curriculum, students are excited about learning.*

—Nasia Butcher, High School Principal

Transforming Learning through 21st Century Skills

The Who Took My Chalk?™ Model for Engaging You and Your Students

Lydotta M. Taylor, Ed. D

The EdVenture Group

Jill M. Fratto, MBA, CPC

The EdVenture Group

Boston   Columbus   Indianapolis   New York   San Francisco   Upper Saddle River
Amsterdam   Cape Town   Dubai   London   Madrid   Milan   Munich   Paris   Montreal   Toronto
Delhi   Mexico City   Sao Paulo   Sydney   Hong Kong   Seoul   Singapore   Taipei   Tokyo

Senior Acquisitions Editor: Kelly Villela Canton
Editorial Assistant: Annalea Manalili
Marketing Manager: Danae April
Production Editor: Karen Mason
Production Coordination: Suganya Karrupasamy
Text Design and Illustrations: Element LLC
Cover Design: Jenny Hart

Photo Credits: Shutterstock, except: page xviii, © Rebecca Devono; pages 2 and 3, courtesy of the authors.

Library of Congress Cataloging-in-Publication Data
Taylor, Lydotta M.
  Transforming learning through 21st century skills : the who took my chalk?™ model for
    engaging you and your students / Lydotta M. Taylor, Jill M. Fratto.
      p. cm.
  Includes bibliographical references and index.
  ISBN-13: 978-0-13-256357-4
  ISBN-10: 0-13-256357-6
 1. Effective teaching.   2. Educational innovations.   3. School improvement programs.
   I. Fratto, Jill M. II. Title.

LB1025.3.T35 2011
371.2'07--dc22

                      2011012491

10 9 8 7 6 5 4 3 2 1   RRD/STP   15 14 13 12 11

ISBN- 10: 0-13-256357-6
ISBN- 13: 978-0-13-256357-4

Contents

chapter 4 *Assess Your School Culture and Environment*   53

chapter 5 *Set . . . and Achieve Goals*   69

January 1, 2011

Dear Teacher,

I see your challenge. Your note to me makes it clear that you know the world is changing dramatically, and you worry that your students are not getting the knowledge and skills they will need. You say you have read Friedman, also some Dan Pink, and recently saw a great animated video of a speech by Sir Ken Robinson on creativity. You just learned that students from Shanghai surpassed all other countries worldwide on the latest PISA exam of 15-year-olds. And you agree with Friedman who tells his own daughters an updated version of the old eat-your-supper-children-are-starving story: "Finish your homework. People in India and China are starving for your job."

You say that your district has been obsessed with meeting state standards. You have worked with the standards and know they are good, but also that the state tests measure basic content knowledge at best. You worry that these standards and even the new Common Core standards, which most states are adopting, are not enough and that your students, even if they master them and do well on the state tests, will still not have the knowledge and skills to compete with students all over the world. They won't have *critical thinking*. They won't have *collaboration*. They won't have *communication*. They won't have *creativity*. And more.

You realize that you will have to expand your curriculum so that your students will experience and then master these 4Cs. You realize you will also need to create classroom assessments, what some call performance assessments, to give feedback to students so they know how they are doing and can become more self-directed learners. There are a lot of new skills that you will have to develop professionally, and you could use some help.

A few school districts have done a lot to define and implement 21st century learning and teaching. These districts provide supports to teachers, including training, coaching, and professional learning communities, and even align their human resources and compensation systems to support these developments. But most districts are either at the beginning of this journey or are not on this path at all.

This poses quite a challenge to you and other teachers who may not have either district-based or school site-based supports for 21st century learning and teaching. But you are determined, nevertheless, to design learning experiences for your students that will engage them and ready them for the work and life in the globally competitive world of the second decade of the 21st century. You are determined to transform your own classroom. You are also willing to collaborate with colleagues to transform your school and even your district.

Authors Lydotta Taylor and Jill Fratto of the EdVenture Group have written this excellent book to pilot you on this journey. They have created a practical guidebook to help you hone your ability to make these changes using their *Who Took My Chalk?*™ model, a multiphase training program designed specifically for educators to help you set the stage for adapting to 21ˢᵗ century learning in your school.

There is much to be done and that you can do, say Taylor and Fratto. You can recognize the need or desire to change; assess your school culture and your personal attitude; set and achieve 21ˢᵗ century goals; communicate clearly to colleagues, parents, and sponsors; predict possible roadblocks; engage internal and external support; make it real in your classroom; and create and finalize your plan for success.

For Taylor, a former teacher, and Fratto, a management consultant, making it real in your classroom is the ultimate goal, but they know well it takes more than new pedagogies to produce a sustained transformation of teaching and learning even in a single classroom. It also takes clear goals, communication, school culture, and support.

Twenty-first-century teaching and learning aims to produce engaged, self-directed, and self-assessing learners. Taylor and Fratto provide excellent examples and resources to support this classroom change. This country is also rich with great practice that evolved in the last decade of the past century and the first decade of the new century. Innovative school models like New Tech Network, Big Picture, High Tech High, Envision Schools, EdVisions, and Expeditionary Learning have blazed the trail, and groups like the Buck Institute of Education and the George Lucas Educational Foundation's Edutopia have provided valuable resources and tools.

As teachers it is our own version of a Hippocratic Oath that makes us do what is best for our students to prepare them for their futures. Let's be ready to do 21ˢᵗ century teaching and learning together with all our colleagues at our school or in our district, but let's also get started and get it right for our own kids in our own classrooms.

Bob Pearlman is a 21ˢᵗ century school and district consultant. He is the former director of strategic planning for the New Technology Foundation, former president of the Autodesk Foundation, and a classroom teacher for 27 years. He can be reached at bobpearlman@mindspring.com and http://www.bobpearlman.org.

preface

Written with the specific challenges of teachers in mind, this book provides you with an overview of 21st century skills and the *Who Took My Chalk?™* model for creating intentional change in your classrooms. Whether you are reading this book because you want to transform your classroom or you are required to read this book as part of a book study or professional learning community, we hope that you will take this time for yourself—to reflect, to create, and to implement new ways to fulfill your goals and reach your students.

We know it is difficult to find the time to read in addition to your daily professional requirements and personal life. We have written this book with that in mind—with easy-to-read chapters and ample opportunity for note-taking and reflection so you can easily follow the steps in this book as you read. Our 35 collective years of teaching, learning, and developing programs with teachers have culminated in this *Who Took My Chalk?™* model, which begins with change management and focuses first on school culture and attitudes and then works outward to setting and achieving goals for school improvement.

To give you an idea of how this book came to be, we thought it would be helpful to share our story with you. Our work together started in 1995, when we partnered to write, and ultimately win, a U.S. Department of Education Technology Innovation Challenge Grant (TICG) that allowed us to educate teachers and community members about the use of computer hardware and software. Lydotta had been in the classroom, teaching math, for more than ten years and had recently started working in the county office to lead the technology efforts of the district. Jill had recently completed graduate studies in business with a focus on information technology.

By 1998 when we won another Technology Innovation Challenge Grant that reached a wider audience, including all the school districts in West Virginia, the focus shifted from technology *training* to technology *integration* into the curriculum. Lydotta's passion for education led her to work in education-focused nonprofit organizations before starting The EdVenture Group in 2001. Our work engaged us with multiple partnerships and funding from organizations such as the Bill and Melinda Gates Foundation, the National Science Foundation, the U.S. Department of Commerce, the Richard King Mellon Foundation, the Claude Worthington Benedum Foundation, as well as other private foundations and school districts.

Our work led us to a connection with the Partnership for 21st Century Skills in 2002; we have focused on creating 21st century learning environments for students since that time. Over time, it became clear that for change to be successful in schools, the most important component was teacher acceptance of the change. Through our work and our own personal growth and development (both of us had obtained coaching and personal development certifications) we realized that when it comes to effective technology integration, it mattered less how much technology or training a teacher had than if the teacher was open to the changes these things would bring to their classroom.

All of these experiences inspired us to create the *Who Took My Chalk?*™ model. The title reflects the question that faces educators today. The chalk serves as an icon of the main tool used in classrooms for years, a tool that has been replaced by technology, resources, and connectedness we could not have foreseen as little as 10 years ago. We believe the *Who Took My Chalk?*™ model reflects a combination of the best of all of those initiatives with an added focus on the individual teacher—his or her goals, attitude, and growth.

Organization of the Book

This book, organized into 9 chapters, introduces and then walks you through the seven steps of the *Who Took My Chalk?* ™ **model**. The first chapter of the book focuses on the **changing world** and why we need to teach today's students differently. The second chapter defines **21st century skills**, provides an **assessment tool for classrooms**, and details the *Who Took My Chalk?*™ **model.** The third chapter looks at **change;** the fourth chapter helps you **assess your school culture** and environment. Chapter 5 addresses **goal setting,** and Chapter 6 focuses on the very important skill of **communication**. Chapter 7 discusses the inevitable **roadblocks** that we face as we move through any type of change and how we can overcome them. Chapter 8 looks at the importance of **engaging support** and how to obtain the support as you move through the change process. Chapter 9 is where it all comes together as the chapter provides you with examples of 21st century teaching and learning that you can apply and **make real** in your teaching environments. At the end of each chapter, you will find reflections and activities to help you as you focus on what you have read, apply it to your own situation, and then take specific actions as you move through the *Who Took My Chalk?*™ model. For those who want to focus on reflections and activities as a group or an entire school, the Book Study Guide provides you with a format for a group **book study**. The appendices include professional development resources for each of the 4Cs: critical thinking and problem solving, creativity and innovation, communication, and collaboration.

Acknowledgments

This book would not have been possible if it were not for the inspiration and support of our husbands and families. Our children have inspired us the most and are the reason we felt so motivated to write this book. While Kayla and Cameron have grown, they inspired us both through our early years of working together. We now look at Ashton and Max and realize that they are the reason this work is so important to all of us.

We appreciate and thank Jennifer Wotring, Kayla Taylor, and Gloria Patterson for supporting and assisting us in this endeavor. Jennifer spent endless hours helping us format and finalize the manuscript.

We would like to express special thanks to our family and friends who are teachers or retired teachers and all of the teachers we have worked with over the years. You are an inspiration to us, and we thank you for the work that you do every day for your students. We send special thanks to the teachers who have participated in our *Who Took My Chalk?*™ workshops. You are the reason we continued our work in this area and created our *Who Took My Chalk?*™ program.

We express our sincere appreciation to Kelly Villella Canton, our editor at Pearson Teacher Education; Annalea Manalili, Kelly's editorial assistant; and Karen Mason, our production editor at Pearson. Their help in putting together this manuscript has proved to be invaluable.

Finally, we appreciate the input from users in the field. Sincere thanks to all of our reviewers: Jo Ann Brandenburg, Hatcher Elementary; Nancy Goodnight, Enochville Elementary School; Kimberly Kludt, Brookings School District; and Allen Martin, Bowling Green City Schools.

Lydotta McClure Taylor, Ed. D

Lydotta M. Taylor is the Founder, President, & CEO of The EdVenture Group, an organization that specializes in change management and leadership programs for education and business. She serves as a national facilitator and chairperson for organizations including The Partnership for 21st Century Skills (P21), the International Society for Technology in Education (ISTE), and school districts across the country. Ms. Taylor earned her Doctorate of Education in Curriculum & Instruction at West Virginia University in May 2011 and is an adjunct professor for the West Virginia University Leadership Studies program.

Prior to founding The EdVenture Group, Taylor served as Vice President for Workforce and Education at the West Virginia High Technology Consortium (WVHTC) Foundation. She completed the Advanced Management Program at Duke University's Fuqua School of Business Executive Education and in 2008 obtained the *Life Success Consulting and Coaching* certification. Taylor began her career as a math and computer science teacher, teaching for 14 years at the secondary level and then as the Instructional Technology Coordinator for the Monongalia County School system. Her love for teaching and learning continues as she works with students, teachers, and school leaders across the country.

Jill Meredith Fratto, MBA, CPC

Jill Fratto is a Certified Professional Coach, accredited by the International Coach Federation and the owner of Enlighten Consultant Services, Inc., a company devoted to helping clients successfully manage significant life or business changes. She has worked as a consultant for The EdVenture Group training, coaching, and creating education programs for the past two years. Utilizing her experience in coaching, business, and education, Jill creates personal and professional development programs for organizations and individuals. Jill earned her MBA from West Virginia University and her coaching certificate from The Institute for Professional Excellence in Coaching (iPEC) in New York. After receiving her certification, Jill served as a Director for iPEC in Atlanta, GA, instructing and developing individuals to become certified coaches. She has written for various publications on topics covering work–life balance, wellness, success principals, leadership, and change management. Jill is passionate about her work in education, empowering teachers to create intentional change that results in positive outcomes for themselves and their students.

The World Is Changing

The World Is Changing

If you are like many teachers, you chose your career to make a difference in the lives of children. You knew that by helping children learn, you could make the world a better place. You enjoy teaching and watching your students learn and grow. It is that enjoyment and passion that pulls you through on the busiest days and carries you through the

many changes you and your students encounter almost daily. The faces of education, technology, and the workforce are changing faster than ever before. Consider the following:

- Today's top jobs did not exist in 2004. (*Shift Happens 2010*)
- By the time today's students are 38, they will have had 10 to 14 jobs. (U.S. Department of Labor 2010)
- In 2006, there were 2.7 billion Google searches. In 2010, that number jumped to 31 billion *per month*. (*Shift Happens 2010*)

The world is changing; our students are changing; our classrooms are changing. As we started working on this book, we reflected on how quickly the world has changed since 1988 as best seen through our own experiences and the experiences of our children.

A Look at the World in 1988

- **Lydotta**

"My daughter, Kayla, is 2. She watches Sesame Street *and has lots of educational toys, but very few are electronic. As a high school math and computer science teacher, I do not have computers in my classroom; the school has two computer labs. Although I don't use technology in my daily routine, I have completed a Pascal programming certificate so that I can teach AP Computer Science."*

Fast Forward 8 Years

- **Lydotta**

"Things progressed over the last 8 years and technology has a somewhat more prominent place in the school and home. My daughter, 10, and son, 8, use Encarta Encyclopedia. They also use Math Blaster and Roller Coaster Tycoon programs. At school, we have added several computer labs for word processing and multimedia applications. Token ring connects the computer labs throughout the building, and many of my colleagues and I have become proficient in using Pegasus, Mosaic, and Gopher."

... and Another 10 Years to the Present

● Jill

"My son, Ashton, is 3. Sesame Street *is still a favorite with children, and he especially enjoys watching Elmo. Like Kayla, Ashton has lots of toys, but the majority of them are electronic. Not only do most toys require batteries, but also they come complete with accompanying websites for games and personalization. At only 3, Ashton has used a cell phone, a computer, an iPod, and his own video player. He uses my computer and asks me to sit across the room and watch him so that he can play the Internet games without my help. He can select some games and intuitively determine how to play them. I don't feel like I had to teach him to do it; he just did it naturally. It's most amazing to watch how many things he can do on his own—even without the ability to read."*

The Disconnect—The Classroom and the Student's Outside World

Many classrooms across the country are home to a variety of technology resources with creative and engaging instruction for students. Conversely, many classrooms look much like they did 10 years ago. Whiteboards or other technology may be in place, but instruction often looks the same. Something is still missing in our education world, preventing it from keeping up with what many children use and experience at home and in their social circles. We believe strongly that this is not a lack of desire or caring on the part of teachers or districts; rather, there are many other factors that contribute to this challenge. These challenges are widespread and evident as millions of dollars are being spent every day to improve education. Instead of researching "common challenges in education today," we asked the experts—you. We asked teachers one question—"What is the greatest challenge you face as a teacher today?" We received nearly 700 responses in only 10 days from teachers representing 30 states of the United States and 4 additional countries. We are sure that we would have had many more in time, but for purposes of this book, we think your responses paint a good picture of the most common challenges facing teachers today. Figure 1.1 is a summary of the responses.

As you can see and are probably not surprised to see, *students* are the chief concern on the minds of teachers. Across the board, teachers most frequently shared their concerns about student apathy, low student motivation, poor attitudes, and discipline problems. Many teachers noted that students' constant access to texting, social networking, and technology was impeding students' ability to complete their work in the classrooms, and many students were bored with standard methods of teaching. Teachers also talked about

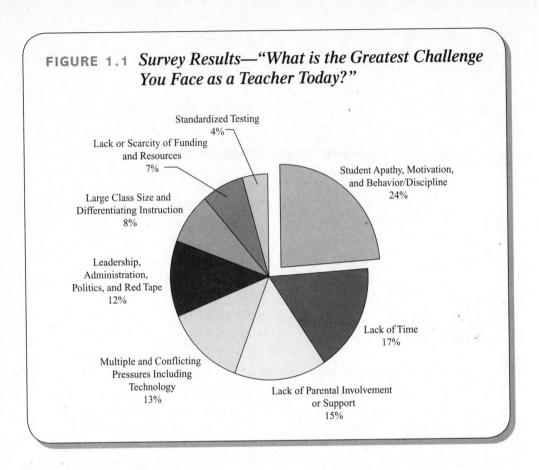

FIGURE 1.1 *Survey Results—"What is the Greatest Challenge You Face as a Teacher Today?"*

the social and family challenges that students bring to school, leading to time spent by teachers listening and helping students emotionally. Although common education challenges like funding, resources, and time were also prevalent responses in the survey, addressing student engagement was clearly the most common response among participants. This is how we categorized the survey results—in order of frequency reported by teachers.

1. *Student Apathy, Motivation, and Behavior/Discipline*

Responses in this category revolve around student behaviors and attitudes as core challenges. Many teachers report that their students are apathetic to learning and education in general. Discipline is also a large concern as many responses in this area relate to the amount of time teachers spend managing their classroom and dealing with student behavior issues. One teacher commented on student engagement and learning—"it seems to be harder and harder for students to let go of distractions. Obviously, this means teachers have to find ways to make that connection. The problem seems to be that many students are totally uninterested in thinking, challenging their own ideas, and reading about or listening to others. I remember this always being an issue, but it seems to be more pronounced with devices like cell phones, iPods, and such taking up so much of their energies." The most frequently used word in these descriptions is *apathy*. Apathy and low motivation in turn lend themselves to poor behavior and attitudes in the classroom. Even when only a small number of students in the classroom are acting out, the distractions impede learning for all students.

2. *Lack of Time*

This category includes all responses that relate to lack of time for teachers to plan, implement, teach, or complete other duties as assigned. It is a common theme for teachers to report that despite staying after school or taking work home, they do not feel they have enough time to fit in all of the mandates required of them. A tight schedule makes it difficult to fit in all the content required by each subject. Many teachers also report a lack of time for planning, collaboration, and creativity—consistently citing the lack of time to complete creative activities with their students due to paperwork and other pressures on their time. "Doing more with less" seems to be a common theme in their responses. Teachers feel that their plates are full, yet more gets added—the expectations are higher, but the amount of time and resources remains the same or decreases.

Teachers report time management as a challenge as they juggle multiple and varied demands on their time during the school day.

3. *Lack of Parental Involvement or Support*

The lack of support, involvement, and communication by parents almost always accompanies a response about student behavior. Many teachers who note student behavior and attitude problems also cite parents as either supportive of their student's negative behavior or unaware of the behavior because they are not involved in their child's schooling (and life in many cases). Getting parents involved in their child's education and being accountable for their child's actions are things that teachers consistently report as a challenge. This is reported by teachers across all geographic areas of the survey.

4. *Multiple and Conflicting Pressures Including Technology*

Increasing pressures from multiple sources; meeting state and national standards, meeting Adequate Yearly Progress, teaching 21st century skills, utilizing technology effectively in the classroom, differentiating instruction, and completing required paperwork are among the pressures teachers cite as concerns in their daily teaching. In this category, technology also plays an integral role as one of the pressures that teachers face. Technology pressures exist on multiple levels including availability, varied levels of knowledge, effective integration in the classroom and (in some cases) students having more knowledge than teachers. To some teachers, the last point may be a factor that impedes them from using technology in their classrooms. For others, they are letting students guide their own learning of technology. Either way, integrating technology remains a challenge that many teachers face.

5. *Leadership, Administration, Politics, and Red Tape*

This category includes responses that focus on leadership challenges, administrative hurdles, and political red tape that make moving forward difficult. The most common comment regarding administration is the feeling that teachers are not heard or supported strongly enough by administrators. These comments most often refer to not being backed up by school leaders in matters involving student issues and discipline and parents' reactions to those issues. Outside of the school, this category includes politics at a state and national level with regard to policies and frequent changes. Lack of communication is also cited as a challenge in this category. Many teachers feel they are often the last to know about changes that directly affect their classrooms.

6. *Large Class Size and Differentiating Instruction*

Responses in this category revolve around the growing number of students teachers have in their classrooms. Teachers report teaching up to 35 students in a classroom at any given time. Educational standards and expectations are the same for all children; therefore, teachers must differentiate their instruction for multiple levels of learners, including students with special needs and students with different cultural backgrounds. The challenge for teachers is teaching to multiple levels in a short period of time while also dealing with discipline and social issues. Teachers also report the need to prepare many students for the learning process and help them overcome negative habits before they can teach mandated content. The overall concern with differentiating instruction is ensuring that all students are getting the level of education and resources they need.

7. *Lack or Scarcity of Funding and Resources*

Simply put, answers in this category are related to the lack or scarcity of funding and resources. Because funding is an obvious challenge in education, it may be surprising to you that this is not higher in our list of reported challenges. We believe this reflects what teachers really value in education—their students. In our experience of talking and working with teachers, the students are the first concern. Most, if not all, teachers would agree that funding is a prevalent challenge in education, yet most do the best with what they have on a daily basis for their students. When it comes down to it, teachers really want to teach and engage their students and want them to achieve success and happiness in life. Funds are certainly needed in education, but students come first to our teachers.

8. *Standardized Testing*

Answers in this category center on the pressures surrounding standardized testing and student results. Responses in this category indicate that education is too focused on the test and show concern that students may not be learning other skills they will need to be well rounded and to succeed outside of school. The challenges related to testing for teachers include feeling pressure about how their students score on standardized tests, finding time to teach everything that will be on the test, and feeling pressured to focus only on test-related materials in their teaching—"teach to the test."

The results of the survey align with what we are hearing when we speak with teachers. Although testing, federal mandates, and funding are significant concerns for teachers, what happens when they stand in front of their students is what is most important to teachers. Our goal in writing this book is to help teachers deal proactively with the challenges of today's classroom and create a better classroom experience for themselves and their students. The difference in our students exists on many levels—the way they think, the way they learn, and the way they see the world. Perhaps this difference is what teachers see when they experience student apathy, negative attitudes, and even behavior issues. We believe if we change our classrooms to fit the ways that our students learn best, we will see improvements in attitude, engagement, and student achievement.

The key reason to make a change in our instructional methods is that we are struggling to keep today's students engaged. No matter where our students live, many of them or their friends text, tweet, and use social networking sites to communicate and share information that we could not have imagined as little as 10 years ago. In too many schools, when these students enter their classrooms, they experience a disconnect between their worlds and the methods and content being delivered. As a result, they become bored or disengaged and do not give their best effort. One teacher summarized this point in her response to the "Greatest Challenge" question—"I think it is children growing up in a society that is SO drastically different from how life was lived 20 years ago. Every house has so much technology and access to information, which has affected them in many ways. Students have shorter attention spans since they do more digital reading, which tends to be in shorter amounts of text, they have so much knowledge at their fingertips just a click away if they want to know something, and they expect to be entertained in a classroom at all times." This challenge will continue as the next generation brings even more skills, experience, and higher expectations for learning to the classroom.

Changing Times Drive Changing Student Needs

The world looks different through the eyes of our children whether they are 2 or 21 years old. The ways they communicate with friends, plan activities, share information, and run their lives are very different from the world that we as their parents and teachers experienced. Even for adults, the world is different now, compared to 10 or even 5 years ago. The pressure is growing for us as teachers to prepare our students for jobs and careers that do not even exist today. Gary Marx, author of *Sixteen Trends … Their Profound Impact on Our Future* (2006), discusses shaping the education system for the future and emerging careers such as artificial intelligence technician, automotive fuel cell battery technician, cryonics technician, leisure consultant, shyness consultant, and virtual set designer.

It is not just the technology that is different for students today, but also their access to information and to the world—a world without limits. Their perceptions, work ethic, values, and viewpoints are different, and consequently, the way that they learn is different. It is not only important, but also imperative that we embrace this changing world and try to understand it so that we stay connected as teachers. Our education systems must reflect our students' world or we will not only miss the opportunity to capture their attention, but also forgo their full potential to learn and grow.

To be most effective in meeting the demands of our future economy and workforce, we must anticipate the development of new careers and shape our education and training programs to meet those needs. Further, we need to make learning a lifelong process that is viewed as engaging and also instills in current students the desire to teach. As changes continue to take place in our world, competition for qualified educators will increase dramatically.

Our world and the expectations we place on ourselves and our students has changed drastically over the past ten years.

The reach of our students extends far beyond their classrooms to countries worldwide because of progress in media and technology.

From a 2011 perspective, we must begin looking at our classrooms as global learning environments. Gone are the days when a student's classroom extended only into the local community. Students today do not see boundaries and will not allow themselves to be limited. It is important to look at the classroom through the eyes of the students. To do that, let us take a look at all of the generations currently in the education system and the workforce.

A Snapshot of the Generations

Depending on your age, you may relate to some of these characteristics. Research overlaps in some cases, but this overview gives you a snapshot of the generations from a work and value perspective. We have based these descriptions on our own research and experience and on the work of Claire Raines, author of *Generations at Work*. You may not think that you fit into one of the generations exclusively, neither do we, but looking at these characteristics helps us understand why generations see and do things differently.

Baby Boomers—Born 1945 to 1964

Baby boomers were born between 1945 and 1964. They tend to be idealistic and career focused. Baby boomers are considered digital immigrants in that they were not born into technology; rather, they immigrated into it as it emerged.

The school setting for baby boomers was one of structure in which students followed and teachers led and provided the expert role of sharing information. Rows of desks were neatly arranged, and often students sat alphabetically and raised their hands to speak. Information was delivered in a lecture format with strict guidelines for behavior and conduct in the classroom. Teachers were most likely very structured, but brought out the best in students for the time and world in which they were living.

Boomers have strong work ethics and prefer schedule and routine, with little room for flexibility. Their expectations are high as they work hard and feel rewarded by a hard day's work. They are dedicated and loyal to their companies and give what it takes. Often, that might mean sacrificing time with the family. The job came first in many cases during the height of baby boomers in the workforce. They are task oriented in that they like to focus on tasks to completion; they were not raised in a multitasking environment.

Generation X—Born 1965 to 1979

Generation Xers were born roughly between 1965 and 1979. They readily accept diversity and change and are known for rejecting the rules. Multitasking is commonplace to this generation because they grew up using some technology and were accustomed to working on several projects or tasks at one time. Gen X students were often latchkey children because many were the children of two working parents or divorced parents.

The school setting for Generation X looked very much like the setting for baby boomers. By the late 1970s, computers were beginning to make their way into schools, but they were very large, were hard to use, and provided few opportunities for those in the classroom. The offerings were limited based on the scarcity of the equipment and the limited knowledge of how to use the equipment and for what purpose. Courses such as computer literacy and basic programming provided the foundation for computer courses in high schools.

Generation X settled into workplaces that were structured much like those of the boomers. However, the workforce was different, and the mindset presented challenges for leaders from the boomer generation. Gen Xers are more independent in the workplace than their predecessors and dislike the rigid and structured work environments. Because of their use of technology and their rebellious nature, they expect immediate and ongoing feedback. The loyalty for Xers is not so much to the company or employer as it is to the work. Unlike the boomers, Gen Xers are comfortable submitting resumes to multiple companies in search of the perfect job and environment. Changing jobs several times over one's career is common with this generation.

Millennials—Born 1980 to 2000

Born between 1980 and 2000, Millennials are primarily children of baby boomers, though some are children of older Gen X adults. They have been called the Internet Generation, Echo Boomers, Generation Y, and the Nintendo Generation. They were born into a technological society of video games, cell phones, digital cameras, personal and handheld computers, and toys that require batteries. As they age and as new technologies are introduced, they embrace the new toys as a way of life—advanced Internet applications, MP3 players, and media-enhanced cell phones, to name a few.

They expect work–life balance and believe they can rewrite the rules. Change is a way of life for them, and they expect it and thrive in it.

Parents of this generation have given all they can to their children and have centered their lives around their children. Many Millennial children have benefited from the resources of their parents and have been given more than any generation before them. This generation has also grown up in a world with more technology, information, and communication than most could have imagined. They have connected with peers globally and enjoy cultural and diversified experiences both socially and academically.

Parents of this generation have offered their children many opportunities and have maintained hectic and demanding schedules to keep up with the numerous available options. Millennials are accustomed to tight and demanding schedules, and they multitask very well to keep up with the demands of extracurricular activities and schoolwork.

In the school setting, Millennial students enjoy and excel when instruction involves action and engagement. Parents of this generation have been strong cheerleaders for their children and often back them in all situations. Millennials have grown up with multimedia entertainment and use it to connect and communicate with their peers. In many cases, the classrooms look similar to those for Gen Xers with additional technology that provides some variety to instructional methods in the classroom.

In the work setting, Millennials want relationships and flexibility. They prefer using technology to assist them with the flexibility and management of their work. This generation wants to build relationships with coworkers; they enjoy working in teams. They interact and create using technology resources to enhance their work. They thrive on flexible work schedules and enjoy a more relaxed work environment.

The Millennial: Take a Walk in Their Shoes

Consider a day in the life of Cameron, a college freshman.

It is 7:00 A.M. Cameron wakes to the alarm on his cell phone. After returning a few text messages, he communicates with friends and schedules his weekend activities through Facebook®. He also uploads from his phone the pictures that he took at dinner last night.

In class, Cameron uses his laptop to take notes, research topics, and create various documents, spreadsheets, and media files. He is also involved in classes that include interaction with students from campuses across the country through video conferencing. He recognizes one of his virtual classmates from Facebook® and instantly sends him a message to let him know they are in the same class. In another class, he uses a clicker to track his attendance and receives a class participation grade based on questions the teacher asks during class collecting electronic responses to track each student's thoughts.

After a club meeting on campus, he gets on his cell phone to send friend requests to peers he just met at the meeting on Facebook® and reads a few tweets. Then he checks his latest test grades on eCampus.

After a late dinner with friends, Cameron uses Skype™ to call his friend in Perth, Australia, who is just getting up for class. They laugh about Cameron's new haircut and share videos from recent social events.

Consider this:

Twenty-year-old Millennials today:

- Entertained themselves with video games for most of their lives;
- Use e-mail, but prefer to Facebook® message and tweet instead;
- Get most of their news and current events through blogs and online sources;
- Expect immediate feedback;
- Enjoy video sites such as YouTube™;
- Use social networking tools to share, manage, and schedule their lives;
- Use the Internet as their main resource for information and communication; and
- Will rarely if ever use a travel agent, a CD player, or a fax machine.

Gen I—Born 2001 to Present

Born after 2001, this generation is just entering the school system, hungry for knowledge and armed with more technical skills and global knowledge than any group before them.

Millennials are accustomed to tight and demanding schedules and multitask very well to keep up with the demands of extra curricular activities and school work.

Not yet formally named, we dub them Generation I—I for immediate—because they are the first generation born into a digital world where information is always accessible immediately. From infancy, they have been surrounded by many high-tech influences and have used many high-speed digital devices. They expect responses from those around them, as quickly as they get them from their computers, sometimes causing them to be seen as impatient. As a generation that has grown up with televisions that rewind, they frequently think that many things in life are the same. This generation is very creative because they have had the outlets to express themselves from a young age. Many feel entitled to have exactly the same as those around them. Opportunities come in many forms because they see no cultural boundaries. They are exposed to cultures, countries, and languages from a young age such that it becomes a part of their everyday life. During their lifetimes, they will engage in many types of education, including online, virtual, and hands-on experiences that have yet to be conceived.

Think back to a day in the life of Cameron, the freshman in college at West Virginia University. Now imagine Ashton's day when he is a freshman in college, considering Ashton's typical day now, at 3.

Ashton wakes up to his own iPod music, "silly songs" imported into iTunes®. He anxiously asks to watch his new DVD, which he can put in and start himself. His portable DVD player goes with him in the car on long trips and on the plane when he goes to visit his grandparents.

Students of Generation I are born into a world of interconnectedness. It is possible and even likely that friends and family followed their birth on Facebook or Twitter.

A Snapshot of the Generations

After spending the morning playing, Ashton calls his Uncle Zack in Doha, Qatar, who was transferred there with his human resource job at a petroleum company. Ashton talks to Uncle Zack through ooVoo.com, a free Internet-based conferencing system that allows him to see Uncle Zack and up to four other users at the same time. Sometimes he sees his friends and family across three time zones. Ashton gets to see and hear Uncle Zack play the guitar and also see Zack's new house and car. Even though he hasn't seen Zack in person for more than six months, it seems as if he sees him every day. When he's hungry for lunch, Ashton asks Mommy to "turn Uncle Zack off."

Ashton is already learning Spanish through his preschool and also through his favorite shows like *Dora the Explorer*™, *Go Diego Go!* and *Sesame Street*®, Mommy's favorite. Although he doesn't grasp the concept yet, he plays with his globe daily and likes to point out where his aunts, uncles, and cousins live.

Since Ashton was born, he has used a computer, the Internet, a cell phone, a Bluetooth headset, a DVD player, an iPod, and of course, he couldn't live without his favorite shows being recorded through DVR. Ashton will never know limits or boundaries. He *assumes* technology, cultural diversity, and communication. How does that experience compare to the experience of our childhood? More importantly, how will their experiences impact our classrooms as they begin their formal education?

Why We Must Teach Them Differently

The challenge for those born prior to the Millennials and Gen I students is determining how to best engage them in the learning process and make the learning process relevant to the world in which they live. We believe that making this connection and helping students see relevance in what they are learning will engage students and alleviate the negative behaviors and attitudes caused by apathy and boredom. The classroom expectations are different—these students want to be engaged, use technology, and work in groups to solve problems and explore the world. Whether we are looking at high school, elementary, or college students, they need an atmosphere that captures their attention. They want to learn, but they tune out lectures primarily because of the many media options available in other parts of their lives. For example, students even at the graduate level admit that as soon as lecture begins, they begin checking Facebook® and e-mail. It is not uncommon to hear a college or high school student discuss excitement for a teacher who engages them in learning, without the traditional lecture and PowerPoint slides. We asked several students about their most recent enjoyable classroom experience.

"My teacher took us outside and let us pick out leaves. I found seven different kinds of leaves—just at our school! Then we used the Internet to learn what kind they were. I can tell you if you want!"

Ashley, First Grade

"My science lab has gone virtual since my teacher introduced iPads in our classroom. We not only work with other kids in our class, but we now work on experiments with kids in other parts of the country. I like using this new tool and can't believe how fun science can be."

Brian, Seventh Grade

"I just finished a DNA Bio lab where I learned 10 times more than I did earlier this week in the lecture on the same topic. The lab allowed me to get involved and learn the concepts by applying them. The lab setting that makes me an active learner is much more effective than being a listener in a lecture session."

Kayla, College Junior

"I like 4 Corners—how we review for a science test. Our class rotates through corners of the room and our teacher rolls a dice to see what corner gets to answer the question. If we get the answer right, we continue. If we are wrong, we have to go back to our seat until no one is left standing. I also like playing Jeopardy to answer questions. The team with the most points gets to choose a prize from the treasure chest."

Abby, Fourth Grade

Today's students enjoy a hands-on, collaborative education environment, where they can question, explore, and discover.

Why We Must Teach Them Differently

Using This Information for Your Cause

If we look at what is most engaging for these students, we can understand why traditional classroom instruction may not inspire every student to do their best. The world looks different for Millennials and Gen I students, as most would agree. We know from our work and from hearing your input that real challenges exist in education today. Some are challenges that we can impact at the classroom level; some are on a larger and even more political scale. Most importantly, we know that you care deeply about your students and want them to leave your classroom prepared for the next level. With this passion and knowledge of how our students think and learn differently, what can you do in your classroom to engage and reach them more effectively? At the end of the day, it is *you* and your teaching style that students remember. Students will not remember "No Child Left Behind" or even perhaps what they scored on a standardized test. Students will remember most the experience they had and what they learned in *your* classroom.

For some students, your classroom is the best place they go all day. Many of you told us in our survey that your students come to school to eat a good meal and feel secure. This is a pivotal time for students. Your role as a teacher is *life long*. Taking the time to think about things differently and go through the process and strategies in this book will empower you with the tools and strategies to overcome some of the challenges you face. As you commit to making change in your classroom, use the knowledge of the generations to motivate you. The new learning styles of the Millennials and Gen I students make it necessary for us to alter and adapt our teaching strategies, our school environments, and our overall view of learning to better engage our students. In the next chapter, we introduce *Who Took My Chalk?*™, an approach that continues to gain momentum. This model provides ideas on what needs to happen in classrooms and what skills are important as we move forward in education.

Chapter Summary

We know that the world looks different through the lens of our students—whether they are in pre-K, elementary, middle school, or high school. As we look at ways they communicate with friends, plan activities, share information, and run their lives, we see that those ways are very different from the world that we as their parents and teachers experienced. Even as adults, we live in a world that is different compared to when we were in school. The pressure is growing for teachers to prepare students for jobs and careers that don't even exist today as depicted by the careers that Gary Marx projected in his book *Sixteen Trends . . . Their Profound Impact on our Future*. We know and have evidence of these changes, and now we must act on them by changing the way we teach. We must build upon the things we are doing well; we need to reconstruct or stop using the strategies that are not working and take our skills and expertise to the next level—creating 21st century learning environments in which our students thrive.

Thinking about both the generational research in Chapter 1 and your own experience since you started teaching, reflect on the following.

• Reflections

1. Why did I choose teaching as a career?

2. How have education and the way I teach changed since I started teaching?

3. How have my students changed since I started teaching?

4. What passion, expertise, and skills do I have that will help create change in my classroom and in my school?

21st Century Skills and a Model for Change

Defining 21st Century Skills

Because we are well into the 21st century, a discussion of 21st century skills is not only timely, but necessary. We believe a large part of the solution to the challenges teachers face in their classrooms and the overarching challenges our education system faces is creating 21st century learning environments where our students can learn, grow, and thrive. The obstacles teachers describe to us and the changes we are experiencing in our world create a substantial need for an education system that challenges and motivates our

students—Millennials and Gen I students with high expectations and limitless opportunities. This shift in schools to teaching and modeling 21st century skills is a learning process that takes *intention*, *time*, *tools*, and *strategies*. In 1998, our consulting firm and partners wrote and were awarded a $7 million U. S. Department of Education Technology Innovation Challenge Grant. The project, *Phase 9*, focused on professional development and laptop distribution. This was a dream project for a teacher. The foundation of the project included a focus on time, tools, and strategies. In 1998, teachers needed *time* to learn how to use technology, the *tools* to use in their classrooms, and *strategies* or lessons and units that were standards based and technology integrated to use with their students.

As we define 21st century skills, it is interesting to look at our beliefs in 1998 about what would help teachers and what we think it takes now to shift to 21st century teaching and learning. We stand on the same foundational beliefs that teachers need time, tools, and strategies to make any large-scale change or integration initiative successful. The results of our recent survey of teachers discussed in Chapter 1 also support time, tools, and strategies as key challenges teachers still face today. After years of working with teachers and creating programs for education, we have added intention to our formula for success. Intention is the act of *determining mentally a specific action*, which we translate as *being open and willing to change*. We believe the foundation for integrating and teaching 21st century skills is *change*. Helping teachers, administrators, and districts open themselves to change and set clear intentions before they do anything else is key to creating long-term sustained results in the shift to teaching and learning 21st century skills.

We have found in our work that the shift to 21st century teaching and learning cannot take place until the school culture is accepting of change and the players involved—teachers, administrators, and staff—are ready and willing to make that shift. So although we see 21st century skills as an answer to the sometimes contrasting school and life environments of our students, we see *Who Took My Chalk?*™ as the model to set the stage for this change to take place. Before we talk about the model, let us be clear about what we mean by 21st century skills.

In our experience introducing 21st century skills to teachers, we find that there are often many questions: What do 21st century skills really mean? How does it change the way I teach my students? How do I begin to understand the skills and what needs to happen in the learning process? As teachers, we deal daily with the reality of a changing world and the impact that 21st century skills can have on our classrooms and the future workplace of our students. Many resources exist to help teachers understand 21st century skills. The challenge is often choosing specific resources to help us best implement these skills in our classrooms.

As we stated, the shift to integrating and teaching 21st century skills begins with setting the stage for change, creating a culture of acceptance for change, and setting intentions for the change to take place. Once that foundation is in place, 21st century skills can be integrated. So what does that look like in your school? For a clear framework of 21st century skills, we partner with leaders in the field to assist us in our definition. In 2002, The *Partnership for 21st Century Skills* (P21) was formed by the U.S. Department of Education and eight companies with an interest in infusing 21st century skills into education. This effort was based on the need for a more 21st century-literate workforce. A framework was created to guide educators as we strive to educate students in the most effective way possible. P21 has clearly defined and set the stage for 21st century skills in the classroom, and we have been involved in that process since P21 began.

● **Lydotta**

"I became involved in the 21st century skills initiative early in its development through partnerships with regional and state organizations. Although the P21 initiative stated many familiar concepts, the approach and the packaging of the effort gave the concepts a new life. I believed that the 21st century skills maps would be great tools for teachers as they integrated technology and new skills into their teaching. In 2008, I participated in the first Professional Development Affiliate Program and in 2009 became one of two facilitators for the Professional Development Affiliate Program. This work allows me to stay connected to others in the education field who share the same passion for growing this effort in schools and districts."

Although we know that P21 is not the only organization that defines 21st century skills, we feel that the outline of the P21 framework provides teachers, principals, and schools a place to start as they fuse these skills into their current instructional practices. Our goal is not to add additional work or requirement to teachers. Our goal is to encourage you and support you in integrating these skills into your current content and instruction.

The P21 Framework

According to the P21 website (www.p21.org), the P21 framework presents a holistic view of 21st century teaching and learning. This combines a discrete focus on 21st century student outcomes with innovative support systems to help students master the multidimensional abilities required of them in the 21st century. In 2010, P21 refocused its description of 21st century skills to provide more clarity on the areas that need to be top priority for all students' learning. The new campaign outlines student outcomes and support systems with a focus on the 4Cs (collaboration, creativity, communication, and critical thinking and problem solving) as key skills that students should use as they learn the content of the 3Rs (reading, writing, and mathematics). The 4Cs represent all of the 21st century skills, and the 3Rs represent all core subjects. The P21 framework makes the concept of 21st century skills much easier for teachers, parents, leaders, and students to relate to and implement because it shows that 21st century skills and content standards are integrated, yet it describes the skills individually to provide clarity. The following is the P21 graphic (see Figure 2.1) used to illustrate 21st century student outcomes and support systems.

As we look more closely at 21st century skills and at the rainbow graphic, it is important to explain the skills in a way that will clearly and simply help us in the classroom. As we have worked with teachers across the country, we have found that many still are not sure what the skills really look like in the classroom. In fact, during our review process for this book, one of our manuscript evaluators stated that she still finds 21st century skills to be somewhat abstract.

The rainbow graphic represents all of the components students must master to thrive in the 21st century and the support systems that promote the outcomes. One of the most

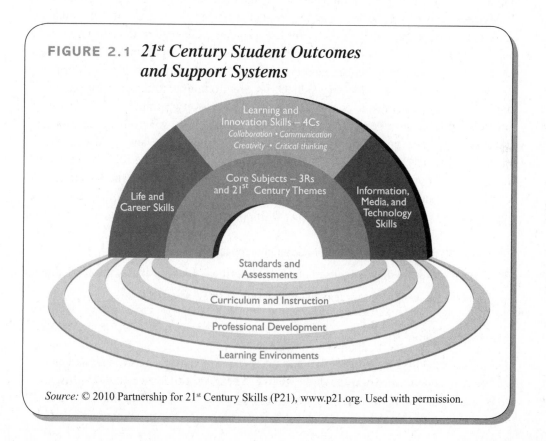

FIGURE 2.1 *21st Century Student Outcomes and Support Systems*

Learning and Innovation Skills – 4Cs
Collaboration • Communication
Creativity • Critical thinking

Life and Career Skills

Core Subjects – 3Rs and 21st Century Themes

Information, Media, and Technology Skills

Standards and Assessments

Curriculum and Instruction

Professional Development

Learning Environments

Source: © 2010 Partnership for 21st Century Skills (P21), www.p21.org. Used with permission.

common misconceptions we have heard in our work is that 21st century skills must include technology. In fact, 21st century skills are often thought to include only technology skills. As you can tell by our examples in Chapter 1, we are strong proponents of technology. We do not, however, believe that technology is a must in every 21st century skills learning opportunity. Although information, media, and technology skills are central to 21st century skills, we believe that students can also be creative, communicate, collaborate, and critically think without technology.

The following is our interpretation of 21st century skills using the rainbow graphic as a guiding model.

Core Subjects and 21st Century Themes

Core subjects and content are at the center of student learning. The core subjects are clearly defined by P21 and refer to the subjects being taught in our schools. This content provides the base for core academic knowledge. Twenty-first-century themes are concepts that should be woven into content. These are concepts that provide a strong foundation for students. They include global awareness; social and civic literacy; financial, economic, and business knowledge; health awareness; and environmental consciousness. In today's world these are prevalent themes that complete a student's knowledge and education. As our view of education evolves, we will begin to see these as lifelong themes and not isolated within formal education systems. The most important thing to note about 21st century themes is that they are not additional subjects we are promoting. Rather, the themes should be integrated with core content. Because it can be overwhelming to think about how to integrate these concepts into your already full schedules, we promote time, tools, and strategies to help do that. In one effort to provide strategies, we developed a suite of courses that help teachers integrate 21st century themes into content. The entire focus behind the development of our courses was to provide content, tools, activities, and resources to help teachers infuse these themes into already existing content. A sample of these courses, all of which tie closely to outcomes in the P21 model, include the following:

- Get Global—a course focused on global awareness
- Critical Think—a course focused on applying critical thinking across the curriculum
- Life Series—a series of three courses focused on integrating life skills

Life and Career Skills

Life and career skills are the skills that will make the student of today stronger and more equipped for the global world in which we live. These are skills such as flexibility, self-direction, personal accountability, goal setting, and leadership. With life and career skills, students are able to better navigate education and career environments. The earlier these skills are developed, the greater a student's opportunities and ability to manage the opportunities and make clear decisions. In our experience with teachers, most feel that they are teaching life skills in some way with their students. Participants in the Life Series courses found that purposely integrating the skills into curriculum yielded even more positive results from their students. Teachers found this course very applicable for the classroom and helpful to them personally.

Information, Media, and Technology Skills

Information, media, and technology skills include the information literacy, the media literacy, and the Information and Communication Technologies (ICT) literacy skills that students need for their learning and work. Teaching information literacy skills means teaching students to access the information they need, determine if it is the right information, and then use and manage that information in assignments and in their daily lives. From tasks as simple as finding a recipe or a concert ticket to researching a problem they are solving in their science class, the world of today's student is filled with many media sources and messages. Students need to learn through our delivery of subjects how to analyze and use the media available as well as be able to create messages using media sources. Teaching ICT literacy means both using and modeling technology with our students. Using technology as a tool to enhance the learning of the core content will create a more engaging environment for our students. Even if some of our students do not have immediate access to computers in their homes today, chances are, wherever they go in the workplace in the future, they will be required to use some form of technology. Being a responsible user and understanding the importance of technology is a *learned* skill today, as we continue to transition to a fully integrated technology society. In the future, it will be an *inherent* skill, considered part of everyday life of our students as they are born into a world that does not know anything other than technology. As we continue to evolve, and especially as our Millennials replace older generations in the workforce, the use of highly evolved technology will be commonplace and expected, rather than learned.

Learning and Innovation Skills—The 4Cs

The 4Cs are the new focus of the P21 rainbow graphic for descriptive purposes, although all of the elements are fully integrated in the process of 21st century teaching and learning. Learning and innovation skills are those being increasingly recognized as skills that prepare students for complex life and work environments in the 21st century. According to P21 and employers in the current workforce, these skills separate students who are prepared for work in the 21st century from those who are not. A focus on collaboration, communication, creativity, and critical thinking is essential to prepare students for the future.

Collaboration, the ability to work together, whether in a classroom or virtually, is a critical skill for today's student. Education and workplace settings are becoming more collaborative as a team approach to problem solving is becoming more prevalent than the once popular autonomous approach to work and education. Students who excel in collaboration will demonstrate the ability to work well with others and use compromise to solve problems and create new ideas and solutions. They assume shared responsibility for projects and outcomes, yet respect and value the individual contributions of the team.

Communication as a 21st century skill means the ability to communicate effectively using verbal, written, and nonverbal communication skills and a variety of tools. Students not only need to be able to articulate their message, but also should be able to do so using various communication tools. Good communicators also exhibit strong listening skills, using listening as a way to decipher meaning and determine values, intentions, and other ideas that are not being directly spoken.

Creativity provides students with the ability to articulate a wide range of new and worthwhile ideas. Creativity also leads to the ability to analyze, evaluate, and improve on old ideas or processes. In the workplace and education settings, the ability to work with others provides endless opportunities where creativity is an asset— being open to the new ideas, being willing to learn new concepts and skills, and

Integrating the 4Cs into core content helps students develop critical skills they will use in higher education and the workforce. Creativity leads to new ideas, problem solving, and continuous progress.

being open to introducing new concepts and ideas to others. As the economy continues to recover, companies are constantly looking for innovative and creative ways to differentiate their companies and products to prosper in the marketplace. Creativity skills are central to this environment.

Critical thinking and problem solving are skills that set apart top-level employees, academics, and entrepreneurs. The ability to solve problems is central to all areas of life and work environments. The ability to reason, analyze, and break down complex problems is critical and supports all of the 4Cs and student outcomes. The ability to look at a problem or challenge and find a creative solution is a defining skill in the 21st century workplace.

It may feel overwhelming to read about all of these skills and concepts and think about integrating them into your current classroom environment. Throughout this book, we will help you create a plan to enhance your learning environment for your students. We will build upon the skills that you are already teaching and help you expand your teaching and learning in all of the categories described here. Today's students will not work in a routine world, but will find themselves in an ever-changing atmosphere that requires all of the 4Cs. The most productive members of our society will be the individuals who can work, play, and live using these skills. According to the American Management Association 2010 Critical Skills Survey, "Critical thinking, creativity, collaboration and communication skills will become more important in a fast-paced, competitive global economy." To grow their businesses, executives see a need for a workforce that is fully equipped beyond the basics of the 3Rs. Executives clearly value these skills and are both hiring and appraising employees based on these critical skills. Employers also indicate that individual evaluations focus more and more on employees' abilities to use these critical skills in the workplace. The entire report may be viewed at www.p21.org.

In Malcom Gladwell's well-known book, *The Tipping Point* (2000), he defines three types of people who are often studied

Education and workplace settings are becoming more collaborative as a team approach to problem solving is becoming more prevalent than the once popular autonomous approach to work and education.

in personal development workshops and in life coaching and success seminars. Gladwell states that "success of any kind of social epidemic is heavily dependent on the involvement of people with a particular and rare set of social gifts." A look at these three types of people and their "social gifts" can help you see how 21st century skills are applied in real life.

1. *Connectors*

Connectors are the people who know a large number of people across different worlds, subculture, and niches. These people, according to Gladwell, have an extraordinary knack for making friends and acquaintances. Because connectors have a unique ability to span many different groups of society, they can bring people together quickly in a way that others cannot. Looking at the 4Cs, connectors are skillful at collaborating and communicating, are most likely creative as they blend into many groups of people, and have diverse experiences.

2. *Mavens*

Mavens are the people who accumulate and share knowledge in a positive and helpful way. They have information about many different products or prices or places, and they want to share it. They want to talk about it and therefore initiate conversations with many people about the knowledge they hold. What makes mavens important is that they know things that others do not and they are readily willing to share this information. They are both the teacher and the student. Of the 4Cs, mavens are the critical thinkers and communicators.

3. *Salespeople*

Salespeople have the skills to persuade others who are unconvinced about what they are hearing. Salespeople draw others into their rhythms and dictate the terms of the interaction. Salespeople have energy, enthusiasm, and charm that can often be contagious to those around them. Salespeople are creative and certainly have strong collaboration and critical thinking skills.

According to Gary Marx, *Sixteen Trends ... Their Profound Impact on Our Future* (2006), the trends impacting our future are endless, but he describes 16 trends with the potential to greatly affect our schools. Although they all are important, we feel that many directly tie to the 21st century skills focus and the 4Cs, thus providing another example of 21st century skills in the real world. Marx discusses the importance of technology and its impact on the speed of communication, the need for continuous improvement and widespread ethical choices, the fact that international learning will become the basic skills, and the pressure to prepare our students for jobs that do not exist. Each of these can be directly linked to one or more of the 4Cs—communication, creativity, collaboration, and critical thinking.

In his 1996 work, Growing Up Digital, Don Tapscott focuses on the "N-Gen" children and how they think. Tapscott discusses the influence of technology and media creating a different mindset that would greatly influence our culture. What motivates these children is very different from what motivated students in the past. Since 1996, technology and media use has grown exponentially, and students' lives seem to revolve around cell phones, the Internet, and social networking. All of these examples help us to realize the importance of changing and adjusting the way we teach children today.

A 21st Century Classroom Assessment Tool

So what does a 21st century classroom or learning environment look like? Unlike the classroom of the past, the "new" classroom does not have one appearance because each classroom will be different. What ties these classrooms together are similar characteristics that support engagement, learning, motivation, and a love of learning. The following will help you begin to formulate your picture of a 21st century classroom. You may come back to these ideas later in the book. The following questions are centered on the 4Cs and relate to your students' experience in your classroom. In Chapter 4, we will talk more about building a school culture that supports 21st century skills in which we as teachers are models for the skills. To each question, you should respond "Yes (Y)," "No (N)," or "Sometimes (S)," depending on the frequency of that activity in your classroom. The questions to which you answer "No" or "Sometimes" are good places to start as you begin thinking about goals in Chapter 5. (You can refer back to this assessment as you set your goals.)

Is Your Classroom a 21st Century Classroom?

Collaboration

1. Do you teach and encourage collaboration and teamwork in your students?　　　Y　N　S

2. Do you have units or lessons that require students to work in teams to complete?　　　Y　N　S

3. Do your students collaborate with you and each other to solve problems and create products or solutions?　　　Y　N　S

4. Do your students assume shared responsibility for collaborative work?　　　Y　N　S

5. Do your students work together as a team, while learning to value the individual contributions of the members?　　　Y　N　S

(continued)

Is Your Classroom a 21st Century Classroom? *continued*

Communication

1. Do your students use a variety of communication skills in your classroom (oral, written, nonverbal)?   Y   N   S

2. Do your students participate in lessons or activities in which listening is a key component?   Y   N   S

3. Do your students openly communicate with you and one another in your classroom?   Y   N   S

4. Do your students share ideas, dialogue, and debate in your classroom?   Y   N   S

5. Is your classroom one in which students feel safe to express ideas and can communicate openly?   Y   N   S

Creativity (and Innovation)

1. Do your students have the opportunity to be open to new and creative ideas from their peers?   Y   N   S

2. Are your students rewarded by you for creativity and "thinking outside the box"?   Y   N   S

3. Do your students engage in creative, activity-based learning in your classroom?   Y   N   S

4. Do your students have a process to create and evaluate new ideas in your classroom?   Y   N   S

5. Do you teach your students to learn from "mistakes," "failures," or strategies that do not seem to work?   Y   N   S

Critical Thinking and Problem Solving

1. Are your students empowered to know how, when, and where to seek knowledge and find answers to questions?   Y   N   S

2. Do your students take an active part in decisions in their learning?   Y   N   S

3. Do your students have the opportunity to analyze and evaluate different points of view?   Y   N   S

4. Do your students engage in activities where they interpret information and draw conclusions?   Y   N   S

5. Are your students engaged in lessons and activities in which they work to solve problems and devise creative solutions?   Y   N   S

Use of Technology as a 21st Century Tool

1. Do your students have the opportunity to use various technologies as tools for learning in your classroom? Y N S

2. Do your students have the opportunity to use many types of media throughout their learning processes? Y N S

3. Do you integrate technology into your curriculum in a way that encourages the use of technology as a tool, rather than a stand-alone skill? Y N S

4. Do your students use computers to help them seek information and gain knowledge? Y N S

5. Do you integrate your students' experience with technology (computers, cell phones, social networks) into your teaching strategies? Y N S

Look at your answers in each category of the boxed assessment tool. In which areas do you have the highest number of "Yes" responses? In which categories do you have the highest number of "No" or "Some" responses? In the categories with more "Yes" responses, 21st century skills are likely integrated into your classroom. In the areas where you respond "No" or "Some" more frequently, that you may want to focus extra work to support and build those areas with respect to 21st century skills. This assessment tool provides you with the opportunity to step back and reflect, which is always beneficial before making intentional change in any area of life. Again, after years of experience in the classroom working with teachers to integrate technology or incorporate 21st century skills, no matter what we have been teaching or for how long, intentional change must be meaningful and important if we are to take the action necessary to make change. In other words, we must be able to see the relevance and importance of teaching 21st century skills in order to be willing to take the steps necessary to change our classrooms and ways of teaching.

Our hope is that the definition of 21st century skills from our perspective and the perspective of the partnership helps you to have a clear understanding of the skills and how those skills are reflected in your classroom. The next step is taking the time to process what and why change is a key factor in this process.

The Who Took My Chalk?™ *Model*

Who Took My Chalk?™ is a model that sets the stage for change. As stated numerous times, our experience has taught us that for change to be effective and sustained, it must first be accepted. The following describes the steps of the *Who Took My Chalk?*™ model as it relates to 21st century teaching and learning. It is important to note that this model can be applied to any change taking place in a professional or personal setting. For purposes of this book, however, we will focus on 21st century skills as the primary change initiative.

Whether we need to incorporate 21st century skills or implement another type of school reform, the adoption of a new set of skills can create confusion and sometimes a less than positive school atmosphere. Many times, schools and leaders are unclear as to how they should begin to change. The uncertainty creates a state of confusion, often leading to miscommunication, tension, and disruptiveness within a school team. Regardless of where you and your school are on the path to creating a 21st century learning environment for your students, you are sure to face change at some point in the process. *Who Took My Chalk?*™ provides a step-by-step model through which schools can progress as they implement change.

If we switch our thinking to the business world, what is often seen during large organizational change initiatives is some level of focus on building team support. Strong companies blend values, beliefs, and a corporate connection. Whether this focus is written, spoken, or merely understood, these companies believe that everyone needs to be on board with the company culture or philosophy to be successful and have productive employees. Employees need to think, feel, and act in alignment with the team. Businesses must change to be successful in this ever-changing world that we have discussed. The secret is in building team support and agreement, giving everyone a chance to participate. Often, this is the missing link when changes are made in the education system.

Who Took My Chalk?™ was created by teachers based on how successful businesses approach making large changes in their organizations. Specifically, businesses hold an off-site training session and bring in an outside facilitator who knows the business, but poses no threat, to help work through new ideas and thoughts, request input, and set a clear path for moving forward. The key is eliminating any threat or concern of repercussions from providing honest and direct responses and feedback. Everyone may not love the new direction, but everyone has the opportunity to discuss and provide input for the new direction. As teachers begin looking at new approaches for 21st century skills, whole school reform, or other recommended or mandated changes, there are often pressures, confusion, and misunderstandings. *Who Took My Chalk?*™ provides a way to help schools work through new approaches and gives teachers a voice in the process. Each school follows the steps of the model at its own pace and in a way that is customized to fit its specific needs. In this book, we progress through the steps not as a whole school, but with a focus on you (the individual teacher) and your classroom. We also use the shift to 21st century learning environments as the example for change taking place in your classroom and school.

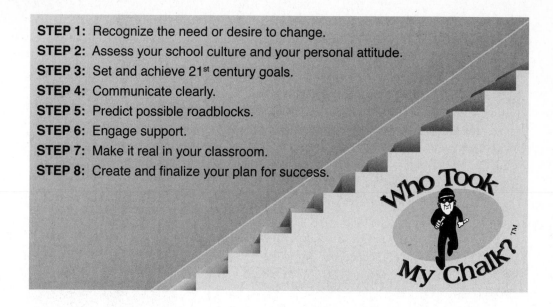

STEP 1: Recognize the need or desire to change.
STEP 2: Assess your school culture and your personal attitude.
STEP 3: Set and achieve 21st century goals.
STEP 4: Communicate clearly.
STEP 5: Predict possible roadblocks.
STEP 6: Engage support.
STEP 7: Make it real in your classroom.
STEP 8: Create and finalize your plan for success.

Step 1: Recognize the Need or Desire to Change

At this stage, you have decided that you either want to change or need to change to create a more optimal situation in your teaching. In some cases, this happens because of new policies or programs that you are asked to adopt in your classroom or school—21st century skills, in our example. You may see the need to change because of the difficulty the school is having in meeting Adequate Yearly Progress. The desire to change could also happen as teachers learn more about the workforce needs and requirements for student readiness in the workplace. In Chapter 1, we looked at the many changes that are occurring in the everyday life of our children. That reality may move you, your colleagues, and your principals to acknowledge the need or desire to change to prepare your students for the future. At this point, it has become evident to you that change is necessary to survive and/or thrive. Change is hard, it is sometimes uncomfortable, and it takes energy; but at this point, you know it is necessary to make adjustments to best deliver education to 21st century students.

Step 2: Assess Your School Culture and Your Personal Attitude

What challenges or opportunities do you want to address? In this step, you give careful thought to your school, its culture, and how that affects you. You assess your own attitude and what is contributing to it (positive and negative). You determine which areas are concerns for you at this time and chart these areas so you can create a visual map of where you want to go.

The first question for each member of the school team is, "How do you generally feel when you walk into your school each day?" The answer to this question tells much about the culture of the school and the attitude of the individual. Now think about how you feel when you walk into your home, a local business, your favorite grocery store, your dentist office, or your church. Comparing and contrasting your answers to how to you feel in different places can tell you much about your personal feelings toward your school. Is it a positive, welcoming place or a place where the energy is low? It is safe to say, most of us prefer to be somewhere that makes us feel positive and happy over somewhere to the contrary. If your answers do not conjure positive feelings about your school or classroom, you may want to look at this area more closely.

This specific step includes other important questions: How accepting do you feel about transforming your learning environments with 21st century skills? How much support do you feel for moving in this direction? How strongly do you feel about the need to make adjustments in your classroom? What are your greatest challenges around creating 21st century learning environments? What factors could change your attitude in this process?

This step in the process gives teachers a voice. When we have the ability to take ownership in the direction and process of the school change initiative, we are much more committed and interested.

Step 3: Set and Achieve 21st Century Goals

From the assessment in Step 2, you will determine which areas are important for you to focus on during this process. This will help you see which challenges you can impact with your goals and which are challenges outside of your control. You will set your goals based on the challenges that you can influence in your classroom. By setting clear goals, you know exactly what you want to achieve, and you have a clear map to follow.

The goals you choose to focus on should help you transform your learning environment for your students and restore, if necessary, your passion for teaching. You owe it to your students and to yourself. We are living in a unique time in education, and we need to progress from what we know and are comfortable doing to leading 21st century skills in our classrooms. You may choose to focus on creating new communication methods for yourself, your students, and their parents. Another possibility could be creating collaboration methods for students that allow them to not only work together within the class, but also branch out to the community and students across the world. You may also choose to focus on transforming yourself to be the classroom leader who is the facilitator of learning, rather than the constant provider of knowledge.

> *Explicitly setting goals can markedly improve performance at any given task. Individuals with clear goals appear more able to direct attention and effort toward goal-relevant activities and away from goal-irrelevant activities, demonstrating a greater capacity for self-regulation. The establishment of clear goals also appears to increase enthusiasm, with more important goals leading to the production of greater energy than less important goals.*
>
> Morisano, Hirsh, Peterson, Pihl, & Shore, 2010

Step 4: Communicate Clearly

Communication is at the heart of the *Who Took My Chalk?*™ process. This step includes creating clear lines of communication in your working relationships with peers, your students, their parents, and administrators. During this step, skills are provided to ease challenges and facilitate good communication within your school team.

Nearly every school we have worked with on this process has determined that communication is an area that always needs improvement. Because the world changes so rapidly, it is imperative that we find ways to keep everyone informed. It is amusing to think back to the days when we thought technology would make our lives easier. Technology creates more avenues for communication and connectedness between people, but does not necessarily create a simpler way of life. We are constantly communicating with our children and our friends by texting, tweeting, Facebooking®, e-mailing, and sometimes calling. With all of these 24/7 communication tools, there is still a lack of communication and information available. This can be a problem for teachers, administrators, parents, and students. When challenges arise within the school, sometimes just talking through the details can clear the air and allow for better communication for everyone. This step in our process is aligned with the 4Cs because it supports communication as a key skill that is integral to the process of teaching and learning 21st century skills.

Step 5: Predict Possible Roadblocks

A roadblock is less likely to bring you to a complete stop if you know that it is there and you can plan another route. At this point in the process, you will look at what could stop you from achieving your goals. By thinking about the possible barriers to success, you can plan ahead so that you have strategies to meet them.

Create a clear plan to focus specifically on your goals and how you want to move ahead. Realize that there may be colleagues waiting to convince you that your ideas will not work and who will try to bring you around to their way of thinking. Be strong in your determination to meet your goals. With your efforts, you may actually be able to transform the learning environments in your school. Ask yourself the following questions and prepare for the barriers and roadblocks that you will face: What could stop you from meeting your goals? What has happened in the past that can help you overcome similar challenges in the future?

Step 6: Engage Support

People who are successful have one thing in common—they get the support they need when they need it. The key questions in this step include the following: Whom do I need to support me in this initiative? What do I need from them? How do I approach them and ask for what I need?

In addition to peer support, what professional development, webinars, or conferences are available to support you in achieving your goals (e.g., attend the ISTE Conference, attend an AP Academy, participate in your state Science Teacher Conference, participate in a webinar or online class, etc.)? It is easier to move forward and make changes when you know you have support. Be diligent in looking for professional development or even coaching that you might need. Take advantage of electronic resources to read and be informed about what others in the field are doing. Today there are a number of blogs, wikis, tweets, and groups with vast amounts of information on specific topics. If you cannot find the area you need support in, create it. Why not? You have valid thoughts and questions, and there are always others who are looking for someone to discuss and support similar ideas. Be creative in the ways you find support and enjoy the learning process.

Step 7: Make It Real in Your Classroom

During this step, we share real classroom examples from schools and teachers implementing 21st century skills, new instructional methods, and activities. You are given examples and resources to either take back to your classroom or modify to meet your needs. This is also the time to look at your current lesson plans and make modifications based on your 21st century goals.

This step is where it really becomes fun. No matter where you are starting from, you will quickly be able to make adjustments to transform your classroom. Your effort might be as simple as assigning collaborative groups to solve a problem using technology tools and resources found around the school using student responders during a reflection period on a novel.

A simple process for self-evaluating where you stand with a current lesson or activity might be the following:

1. What actions do your students take during the instruction time of the lesson or activity? Specifically, are the students collaborating, creating, communicating, or critically thinking?

2. Are the students engaged or simply taking notes on the information you are providing?

3. Are your students aligned in perfect rows with little movement or interaction?

4. Are your students excited about what they are learning?

5. Are you and your students having fun?

In this step you can help your students find the joy and excitement in learning and solving problems. In Jim Haudan's *The Art of Engagement* (2008), he states that "people work because they have to. That's why they call it work. But people engage because they want to. When students are disengaged, the learning process is merely work. Yet when the students can see the link between the learning process and their future, they engage because the task is personally important." In addition, High and Andrews in *Engaging Students and Ensuring Success* (2009), say, "What is needed are teachers who know how to create, as a matter of routine practice, schoolwork that engages students. Schools cannot be made great by great teacher performances. They will only be made great by great student performances. To have those student performances we must engage the student in learning." These comments give us something to think about as we embark on this step of making these skills real in your classroom.

Step 8: Create and Finalize Your Plan for Success

Because every teacher is different, the plan for success will also be different. In this step, you will design your plan and all of its components based on the previous steps. At the end of this book, you will have a complete plan and a solid starting point to begin transforming your classroom environment and teaching strategies to align with the appropriate changes for your classroom. In this step it is important to remember that any individual or group making intentional change, that is, creating 21st century learning environments, must be patient and focused. The idea of being transformational, taking the lead toward a common vision and causing change, applies directly to this situation.

Now that we have laid the foundation for the *Who Took My Chalk?*™ model, you will proceed through each of the steps of the model in each chapter that follows. The most effective way to use this book and be most successful is to complete the activities at the end of each chapter. This will provide you with a personalized working plan you can use as you teach and model 21st century skills in your classroom.

Chapter Summary

The shift to integrating and teaching 21st century skills begins with setting the stage for change, creating a culture of acceptance for change, and setting intentions for the change to take place. Once that foundation is laid, 21st century skills can be integrated. The *Partnership for 21st Century Skills* has clearly defined and set the stage for 21st century skills in the classroom through the 4Cs—collaboration, creativity, communication, and critical thinking and problem solving.

Who Took My Chalk?™ is a model that sets the stage for change. The eight steps of the model include the following:

Step 1. Recognize the need or desire to change.

Step 2. Assess your school culture and your personal attitude.

Step 3. Set and achieve 21st century goals.

Step 4. Communicate clearly.

Step 5. Predict possible roadblocks.

Step 6. Engage support.

Step 7. Make it real in your classroom.

Step 8. Create and finalize your plan for success.

• Reflections

After answering the questions in the 21st Century Classroom Assessment Tool, respond to the following:

1. What did you learn from the assessment? How were you surprised?

2. In which of the five areas did you have the most number of "YES" answers? "NO" answers?

3. In which areas were you strong? How can you build upon what you are doing well?

4. On which areas will you focus most effort as you begin the shift to modeling and teaching 21st century skills in your classroom?

Reflecting on the eight steps of the *Who Took My Chalk?*™ model, respond to the following:

1. What were your first impressions of the model?

2. What do you hope to obtain from the model as you progress through the steps in this book?

chapter 3

Recognize the Need or Desire to Change

Defining Change

The first step in the *Who Took My Chalk?*™ model is recognizing the need or desire to change. In the context of creating 21st century learning environments, recognizing the need to change is part of the foundation described in Chapter 2 during the discussion

about *intention*. We know there are challenges in our classrooms that we want to address, and we know that our students need to be engaged or *re*-engaged in their education. To make change, we must first intend for that change to take place. This intention to change serves as a building block or foundation for the *Who Took My Chalk?*™ process. Change is a simple term that we use on a regular if not daily basis; but what does it really mean?

Change can be defined as altering, making different, or causing to pass from one state to another. Change allows us to continually grow both personally and professionally. If we do not grow, we may find ourselves stuck in our comfort zones where we are less willing to try new strategies or make conscious changes in the way that we teach. Change can also be referred to as turning off our autopilot and looking at things through a new set of lenses.

All of these definitions align with what most of us think about when we define change, but most of us rarely reflect on what change means and the role that it plays in our daily lives. Although it is sometimes easy and comfortable to be a creature of habit and maintain the status quo, we like to focus on *growing* as the key component and driving force of change. We believe that when we look at change as growth, it is easier to accept because everything grows. Instead of alterations or upheaval, we see change for its opportunities and positive aspects on our personal and professional lives. The challenge for most is purposely *applying* change in our lives.

We acknowledge that many of you enjoy change and make changes and adjustments daily in your personal and professional lives. We know that many engaging, forward thinking, 21st century skills-related activities happen in your classrooms. Later in the book we will look at several examples of this good work that is happening. We know many of you are collaborating and building new opportunities for your students' learning every day. Our goal for this chapter is to help you take that one step further. We want to encourage you to step out of your comfort zones and try new things, regardless of where you are on that spectrum. We believe it is imperative that we continually grow, change, and become better. So, as you read this chapter, know that we applaud your successes and encourage you to continue growing and building upon what you are doing in your classrooms.

As both of us have experienced opportunities in our careers, we have found one of the most effective—though often difficult—ways to deal with change is to embrace it. By doing so, we have found that adjustment comes easier and more quickly than when we struggle or resist. Many times, we take advantage of opportunities or even make them happen because we want to grow and stay excited about what we do every day. By growing, we stay in a more positive mental state. It is important to stay motivated and excited about life and our daily activities. In fact, we believe that these things keep us positive and happy on a daily basis. Without change, we may end up in a stale or boring routine. This happens all too often to those of us in the classroom. The nature of the job as we know it often lends itself to doing the same thing year after year with only new students to greet us. Having been in the classroom and still teaching today, we realize that it takes special focus and effort to grow and build new techniques and methods for 21st century learners.

If we think about the habits we develop as we go through our daily routine, we realize that it is necessary to focus consciously on doing some things differently to create change and growth in our life. Many times, our predisposed notions of how things *are* limit us from dreaming about how they *could be*. For example, when Lydotta was six years old, she knew she wanted to be a teacher.

● **Lydotta**

"I remember asking my parents for a chalkboard, and I remember exactly where it hung in our basement. I played school with my brother and sister daily. I loved lining them up in chairs and writing on the chalkboard. Their full attention was on me, the teacher. I loved my pretend role and knew that teaching was what I wanted to do."

This vision of being a teacher stuck for many years and may sound familiar to you. As a high school math teacher, Lydotta stood at the chalkboard and worked math problems, dusted off her hands, and helped her students one by one. This vision of teaching sticks with many of us because we tend to teach as we were taught. This method of teaching was effective for the time, but even then students enjoyed different methods of delivery. Deciding to approach our delivery differently often creates an unsettled feeling that we call the *fear of change*. This is especially true in our classrooms when we face 25 to 36 students and the related daily occurrences. It is often easy to change something in our personal lives when we have to focus only on ourselves. It is a bit more challenging, but still feasible, when we think about our classrooms. We encourage you to address this fear of change by thinking of expanding on the positive aspects of your classrooms.

Before we begin talking about making changes in your classroom, take a moment to reflect on the teaching strategies and systems in your classroom that are working. After completing the quiz in Chapter 2 about 21st century learning environments, you probably learned that there are specific areas where you are strong. We know that some things are working, and you deserve to commend yourself for a job well done in the areas where you excel. Now, with the confidence of knowing that you are doing well in some areas, think about the areas you can build upon. How would your classroom be different if you were maximizing all of the areas of the P21 rainbow graphic in your teaching strategies? What would you be doing differently? How would your classroom look? How would your students be learning and interacting?

Why is it important for us to make changes in the way we teach? Even the areas where we are strong can be improved and taken to the next level. Think back to the examples in Chapter 1 about our changing students and the concept of our ever-changing world. To thrive in the society in which we are living we must make adjustments. We must also make adjustments to help our students thrive in the society in which they are growing. Our students must learn to embrace change and understand that their futures will demand change. As teachers, we must ensure that we are motivating and engaging our students so they can achieve success in gaining the knowledge and skills they need for *their* workforce. By doing so, we can feel a sense of satisfaction for a job well done. For most of us, that is the reason we entered the teaching profession in the first place: to make a positive difference in the lives of children.

We hope you are at some level of agreement with this discussion and our thoughts on change. You may still have questions about where to start and how to know if the time is right to begin making changes for you and your students. We suggest that the time is always right and that the time to begin is now. Whether you start in your classroom implementing one of the 4Cs or using a new technology tool or you decide to start on a schoolwide initiative, the time is *now*.

For many teachers, making a difference in the lives of their students is at the heart of their career and day-to-day motivation.

Common School Scenarios that Call for Change

Although our primary focus in this book is on the shift to 21st century teaching and learning, we see many common scenarios in our work where schools have decided or are required to make significant adjustments for the success of their students. These scenarios may be the first steps in moving toward 21st century learning environments. The sample scenarios often call for a decision to make alterations that move the situation forward in a positive way. Many of the scenarios described focus on school culture, which will be discussed in Chapter 4. The following are real scenarios that may challenge schools and call for change management support. These scenarios also impact teachers and their classrooms. We have seen these time and again within schools where we have implemented the *Who Took My Chalk?*™ model.

Widespread Policy Reform

If your school is implementing a widespread policy change, there are often many changes at the classroom level as well. Significant changes to policies or to the way things are done in the school often affect attitudes, procedures, communication, and many other elements of the school. As a teacher, you want to know how you are affected and what steps you need to follow for smooth implementation.

Change of Administration

Perhaps a new principal has just been appointed to your school. As a teacher, you know that new leadership means learning new processes and new ways of communicating. This time of change provides the opportunity to deal with issues and work together for the changes that are needed to provide a more positive learning and working environment.

Adoption of New Technology

If your school is implementing a new technology application, this may cause emotions ranging from frustration and confusion to excitement, depending on your comfort level with technology. We have found that adopting new technology is about not only providing training, but also creating buy-in as to how the technology will support you and make instruction more engaging and meaningful for your students.

School Mergers

School mergers are challenging even in the best of situations. Mergers typically result in uncertain feelings, turf issues, loss of identity, and communication issues. Creating a process to give every teacher a voice and an opportunity to feel ownership in a new team can build a strong foundation to support this type of change.

Adoption of a New Schoolwide Curriculum or Program

Another area that can often be overwhelming, but is prevalent in schools today, is the adoption of a large-scale program. Imagine that your school has been asked to adopt a new program that requires significant changes in every classroom in your school. Maybe it is the implementation of a new reading or math program, a new discipline policy, or the implementation of 21st century skills. Whatever the new or changing program, it can be overwhelming for everyone involved. It is not uncommon for this type of alteration to cause issues among the staff, leadership, parents, and students.

These examples just scratch the surface of scenarios that stimulate the need for change with a focused team approach. For years, schools have been forced to deal with change without much time to focus as a team and get buy-in from everyone. As we focus on growth for the 21st century and the ever-changing world we live in, it is important to think about and act upon ways to make change the most effective and engaging for everyone involved. Many of the examples above go hand in hand with the shift to 21st century learning environments. The changes that occur through an intentional focus on change and growth in our classrooms will greatly impact the way we teach and adopt 21st century skills into our teaching strategies.

Positive Change Starts with a Positive Attitude

As you reflect on your school and your experiences, you can either relate to these scenarios or think of others that have occurred at your school. What have you experienced in times of school change or transition? How did your school handle these situations? How could the situation have been handled better? We believe that the success of any school transition begins with attitude—your attitude and the attitudes of everyone in the school, beginning with the teachers and leadership. As a starting point, we suggest looking closely at your own attitude and how you respond to changes. This suggestion

Maintaining a positive outlook even when others around you are not can be difficult, but comes with rewards in the long term.

is not intended to imply that you or your colleagues have a bad attitude. We simply think that looking first at ourselves is more effective than trying to change others. By consciously considering our attitudes as we respond to change, we have a more objective and positive lens for accepting and recognizing what needs to change or grow in our lives.

Attitude can be defined as your thoughts, your feelings, and your actions. Your thoughts determine your feelings, and your feelings determine your actions. As a former math teacher, it is logical to look at this as an equation:

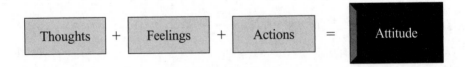

$$\boxed{\text{Thoughts}} + \boxed{\text{Feelings}} + \boxed{\text{Actions}} = \boxed{\text{Attitude}}$$

We rarely have time to reflect or consider what attitude means or what causes our attitude to change. Attitude begins with our thoughts. The way we talk to ourselves and interpret events will create our thoughts. These thoughts are powerful, and we often do not realize that we are allowing our "self-talk" to affect us. Self-talk occurs based on our past and the way that we have learned over time to interpret events. A student forgetting his homework, a traffic jam that makes you late for school, a comment from the principal, lack of time to grade papers, or a disgruntled parent could create thoughts that significantly impact our attitudes.

This self-talk turns into a set of feelings that we perhaps unknowingly help determine. If we can keep our thinking positive regardless of the situation, then our feelings will remain positive. If we can think positively, we will *feel* the same way. This is not always easy to do, but just by being aware of your thinking, you can begin to control how you feel. Control and focus are important because the feelings you have create your actions. Your actions greatly affect your day and everyone around you. Your actions can influence a positive attitude in a negative way.

George Bernard Shaw was noted for saying, "Better keep yourself clean and bright: you are the window through which you must see the world." Psychologists refer to this as the "Broaden and Build Theory of Positive Emotions." Barbara Fredrickson developed this theory to explain the mechanics of how positive emotions are important to survival. If we apply this to teaching, the "clean and bright windows" will be obvious to our students and positively impact the way that they perceive school. Those same windows will help teachers deal with issues and build a more positive culture. Too often, the school system, general life challenges, students who need extra help, and other internal and external challenges can quickly impact teacher attitude and how they face each day. For the sake of the teacher, the student, and the school, all of us need to have "clean and bright windows" for the best delivery of education.

By focusing on your thoughts, you realize that much of your thinking has an impact on your attitude and how you respond to situations. Consider this example.

It is early morning before school and you are running late. Your oldest child can't find his shoes and your youngest doesn't like what you packed in his lunch. When you finally do get in the car and on your way, you get held up in traffic with your children arguing in the back seat. By the time you get your kids to school and then get to your own school and classroom, you are late.

It would not be surprising to feel stressed and in a not-so-positive state of mind at this point. Sometimes, when you have a day that begins this way, you find yourself saying, "It's been one of those days." Before you know it, it turns into one of those days because you cannot seem to get your mind back into a positive state. Your original negative thoughts about the morning routine can lead to stress, anger, and resentment. These thoughts can cause your own actions to be negative (complaining to peers or being short with students), which only start the cycle over again with new negative thoughts.

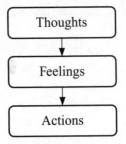

Look carefully at how you respond to situations and determine if you allow circumstances to control you. By simply taking a deep breath and stepping back from the situation, you will find that you walk into your day with more positive thoughts, thus starting a positive thought-feeling-action cycle rather than a negative one. We're all human, and we all experience these challenges, but if you can be conscious of what is happening in your thoughts, it can really make a difference. A good example of this comes from one of Jill's coaching clients.

● **Jill**

"I was working with a client who was describing a 'bad day,' which escalated to the point of a confrontation with another driver while on the road. My client was describing how awful the day had been and I stopped her. I asked her what message she had been giving herself that day (What was the predominating thought?). She laughed as she remembered that she kept repeating to herself, 'This day just keeps getting worse and worse.'"

With this thought in her mind, she then began to look for bad things to happen. Our thoughts create our feelings and moods, which, in turn, help create the events in our lives. The point in this example is not to say that we are to blame for bad things that happen to us; rather, we do contribute to the events in our lives through our thoughts and feelings.

This tactic works well when you feel like your mind is racing or you are feeling anxious or nervous about something. Stop and ask yourself, "What is the main thought I am having about all of this?" For example, when things seem to be piling up and you feel like you can't get it all done—perhaps at the beginning of the school year or right before standardized testing—the main thought might be, "I am overwhelmed" or "I can't do it all." This core thought leads to a feeling of exhaustion or anxiety, which can lead to no action or negative action such as making mistakes or missing deadlines.

At times the result (or action) can even be physical—panic attacks, exhaustion, and so forth. By asking yourself what you are telling yourself and becoming aware of the answer, you stop repeating it needlessly. In this example, by realizing you are saying, "I can't do it all," you can replace that with a positive thought such as "I am accomplishing everything that I set out to do today." This awareness and proactive approach to reversing a negative pattern will help you regain your sense of balance and feel good about what you are able to accomplish.

Teachers rarely have breaks in their days and find the days filled with constant interaction with students, colleagues, and parents. This makes it hard to stop and think about your attitude, but we believe it can have a positive impact no matter what you do or where you work. William Penn is known for saying, "The secret to happiness is to count your blessings while others are adding up their troubles." Over 2,000 years ago Epictetus said, "We are disturbed, not by the events of our life, but the views we take of them." This statement, made years ago, pointed out the importance of the views we take, yet many of us still struggle with maintaining a positive outlook today.

Research that studies the links between thoughts or mental activity and health and life outcomes has increased significantly over the past few years. A recent Google™ search for positive attitude + life outcomes returned 2,820 specific hits that include both terms. This tells us that there is a significant correlation between the two. Many of the resources that we found focus on our health-related life outcomes and the power of positive attitude. Numerous studies support that having a positive outlook has positive outcomes both mentally and physically. Researchers have found that people who see the glass half full and think positively are generally happier than those who see the glass half empty. You can feel it when you interact with people and can typically determine how those you work and interact with see the world. Lydotta fondly thinks of a friend and teacher colleague who stands out in this area.

● Lydotta

"I met my friend, Pam, standing at the registration desk for new teachers my first day of teaching. We instantly hit it off as we were both new math teachers. Today she is an adopted aunt in our family. My children quickly learned her favorite comment—'I thoroughly enjoyed myself.' No matter what she was facing, she always managed to bring a positive attitude. She maintained this attitude over thirty years of teaching middle school math. She is proof that it can be done."

Thinking positively makes us feel more important and more connected with our purpose in life. This doesn't happen easily every day, but those who focus on the positives and seeing the bright side as a routine way of thinking have better days in spite of the circumstances.

Following the death of Christopher Reeve, Carol Ryff, psychology professor at the University of Wisconsin–Madison, stated, "There is no doubt in my mind his positive attitude extended his life—probably dramatically. There is a science that is emerging that says a positive attitude isn't just a state of mind. It also has linkages to what's going on in the brain and body." The same article cites Kiecolt-Glaser, a clinical psychologist at Ohio State, saying, "In laboratories there are lots of easy ways to make people depressed or anxious for a long period of time. It's harder to make people happy" (Jayson, 2004).

The question then becomes—how do you create and protect your positive attitude? Lydotta remembers a conversation she had with a hotel employee in the breakfast area a few years ago.

> ● **Lydotta**
>
> *"I remember complimenting a hotel employee as she cleaned up a terrible mess a group of young children had left on a table. To my surprise, the employee responded, 'Honey, they didn't give me my happiness and I'm sure not going to let them take it away from me.'"*

This kind of attitude makes a lasting impression on people, as it did in this case. It serves us all well to not let others, whether it is our families, students, principal, peers, or strangers, take away our positive thoughts. Positive thoughts create positive feelings, and our actions follow. You have been around people who follow this process daily no matter what happens. Staying positive takes a conscious effort, some days more than others, but with consistent positive thinking, you will notice the positive difference in your life just by creating positive thoughts.

The benefit to positive thinking is that you will also notice the impact your attitude has on the people around you. For example, if you walk into school focused on your positive thoughts not allowing anyone or anything to take those feelings away, you will notice that your colleagues and students begin to reflect this way of thinking. Think about places you go where you feel welcomed and warm. Our guess is that those places are filled with individuals who focus on positive thinking and customer service. Think about your grocery store, doctor's office, and bank; which ones make you feel good? Do you think the individuals who welcome you are positive? Now ask yourself how often do you really apply this thinking in your classroom. Research has shown that habits are more likely to develop after you apply a behavior for 21 days. Repetition and focus are the keys to help you create and maintain this behavior. Based on this, make having a positive attitude your priority for 21 days. We realize it will not cure everything, your child won't always find his shoes or like his lunch, but your thinking and attitude will be more positive and people will notice, especially your students. Build on the positive thoughts you have based on the

Students benefit in a learning environment where the attitudes and atmosphere are positive.

good things you see in your students and school. Taking the time to notice and focus on those things will help you as you begin your 21-day positive attitude priority.

No matter where we are in our lives or careers we all need reminders of the importance of keeping a positive attitude. Everyone can benefit by focusing on his or her attitude. John Maxwell, a well-known leadership author, discusses the importance of attitude in his book *The 21 Indispensable Qualities of a Leader* (1999). Maxwell's 13th quality, positive attitude, "If you believe you can, you can," points out four areas to consider: "Your attitude is a choice, Your attitude determines your actions, Your people are a mirror of your attitude and maintaining a good attitude is easier than regaining one." Teachers and principals are all leaders within their schools, and these leadership suggestions apply to all of us. Everyone in the education system is a leader and role model for children. Be sure to consider how well you are applying these in your classroom and in life. By creating a conscious awareness of these thoughts, you can significantly impact the attitudes in your classroom.

A Look at Our Fears

In addition to assessing your attitude, it is also important as you embrace change to look at what might be holding you back. What are your unspoken fears? Often, as much as we hate to admit it, fear is a major factor that slows or even stops us from making positive change and growth in our lives. This can also be described as stepping out of our comfort zones. We all get comfortable with our environment, our classrooms, our schools, and our homes. Asking people to step out of those comfort zones is sometimes a big request,

especially when they have been successful year after year. The concept behind the title—
Who Took My Chalk?™ —is that technology and other tools are replacing the iconic
piece of chalk many of us have used in our classrooms. When we think about stepping
out of our comfort zone and changing the way we teach, fear is not uncommon. What if I
fail? What if this new implementation of collaborating and critical thinking doesn't work?

As we thought about the reality of this and imagined what fears our readers would
have, Lydotta reflected on an example of stepping out of her own comfort zone while in
the classroom:

> ● **Lydotta**
>
> *"I remember when I volunteered to teach computer programming at my high school. I had been
> teaching a variety of math courses for about 3 years. I was comfortable in my job and was very
> happy teaching mathematics. I had taken a few computer science courses in college, but I was
> brand new to the Pascal language. Despite my lack of knowledge, I agreed to take on the challenge
> to teach the new course. I learned the language doing my best to stay ahead of my students. I
> realized I was not in my comfort zone in the computer science classroom. My students were very
> engaged and seemed to love solving the problems and debugging the programs. I was so busy
> working hard to stay ahead of my students that I began to lose my excitement for the class. Then
> one day it dawned on me that I didn't have to be the expert. I needed to provide information and
> the opportunity for them to solve the problems. We as a group could collaborate, think critically,
> and communicate to figure out problems and issues. It was in this computer science class that I first
> experienced the 'teacher as facilitator' approach to teaching."*

As a teacher, you have probably had experiences similar to this example. Reflect on
times when you have had similar experiences or passed by an opportunity to step out of
your comfort zone. Embracing these situations and serving as a facilitator can increase
student engagement in our classrooms. Serving as a facilitator allows us to continuously
step out of our comfort zones and become better teachers. What other examples can you
think of where you would benefit from stepping out of your comfort zone?

Making the Intention to Create Change

We have provided you with a number of different thoughts on change that should help
you understand how you respond to and deal with change. There are many different
responses to change, and no two people will handle the same challenge in the same way.
Reflect on the thoughts from this chapter. What role are you ready for in the change
process? Are you already the positive thinker who makes alterations to find the best way

to deliver instruction to students? Are you more the person who is just getting started in adopting new ideas and delivery methods in your classroom? Wherever you are in the implementation of 21st century learning, embrace your position and take steps to move forward. Setting the intention to make positive change in your classroom will provide you with a solid foundation to successfully follow the steps of the *Who Took My Chalk?*™ model. We will help you set goals in later chapters and determine what you want to change as you step out of your comfort zone and create a 21st century classroom that provides new challenges and learning opportunities for your students.

Chapter Summary

If we think about the habits we develop as we go through our everyday routines, we realize to create change and growth in our lives it is necessary to focus consciously on doing things differently. Many times, our predisposed notions of how things are limit us from dreaming about how they could be.

Why are you reading this book? Did you want to make a change, or did something change in your environment that brought you to this point? Think about the common school scenarios that call for change. Are any of those affecting your school right now?

● Reflections

1. Assess your attitude by answering the following questions. What is my overall attitude while I am at school? What types of conversations do I engage in with colleagues? How do my attitude and related moods affect my students? How can I tell?

2. Looking back to the "thought-feeling-action" cycle, what habits have you developed in your thoughts that are contributing to your feelings and resulting actions?

   • What are you telling yourself?

- How does that make you feel?

- What do you do or how do you act as a result?

3. What kinds of change do you *intend* to create in your classroom?

4. What kinds of fears surface for you when you think about changing your teaching style or your classroom?

5. How can having a positive attitude help you overcome those fears? What other things might help push you out of your comfort zone and help you overcome any fears you have about implementing 21st century skills into your curriculum?

chapter 4

Assess Your School Culture and Environment

What Is School Culture and Why Is It So Important?

A recent Google search for "school culture" returned 573,000 hits. Ironically, if you ask most teachers, the topic of school culture and its importance is often overlooked in staff meetings and professional development at their schools. The education challenges of the

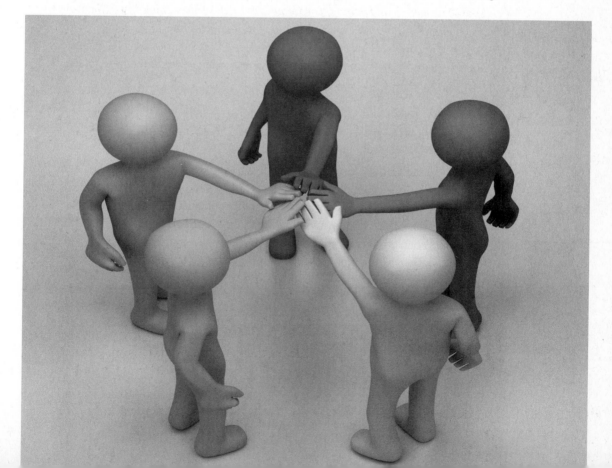

21st century coupled with the lack of time for connecting with peers during the school day make teacher stress levels higher than ever. It seems that the system has failed to address the key element that can build a strong foundation for the overarching pressures schools are facing—school culture.

One of the clearest definitions of school culture that we found is from Gary Phillips (1993), who describes school culture as the "beliefs, attitudes, and behaviors that characterize a school in terms of: how people treat and feel about each other, the extent to which people feel included and appreciated, and rituals and traditions reflecting collaboration and collegiality." Most schools do not dedicate or have enough time to focus on these characteristics or give teachers the opportunity to address issues to improve the work environment. Many teachers feel that their voices are never heard and there is an overall lack of communication around school culture.

If we switch our thinking to the business world, we find a similar definition of culture:

> *Corporate culture is a blend of the values, beliefs, taboos, symbols, rituals and myths all companies develop over time. Whether written as a mission statement, spoken or merely understood, corporate culture describes and governs the ways a company's owner and employees think, feel and act. The culture could consist in part of a corporate symbol, like the rainbow-colored apple that symbolizes Apple Computer. Whatever shape it takes, corporate culture plays a big role in determining how well a business will do.*

(Entrepreneur, n.d.)

The habit of remembering and keeping a focus on the importance of culture often sets successful companies apart from their competitors.

During our years of working in and with schools, we have learned much about how students, teachers, and administrators work together in the learning environment. Using this experience and our current research, we have defined school culture by what is most effective for 21st century teaching and learning. The following six characteristics define positive school culture and support 21st century teaching and learning: student engagement, collaboration, goal setting, action planning, assessing attitude, and engaging openness.

Six Characteristics that Define Positive School Culture

The first characteristic is the level of **student engagement** in the learning process. A positive school culture provides an engaging learning environment for students.

Students are motivated, actively engaged, and excited about the activities taking place in their classrooms. The teaching methods and overall climate of the schools contribute to an engaging 21st century learning environment for students and teachers.

The second characteristic focuses on **collaboration**. If principals and teachers have the ability to work together to determine and prioritize challenges and opportunities within the school, issues can be addressed to improve and maintain a positive school culture. This characteristic looks at how well principals and teachers utilize or create opportunities to share positive and negative aspects of the school. This characteristic is central to creating a positive school culture or a positive culture with any group of individuals. Thousands of workshops are held every year focusing on teamwork and collaboration. Collaboration does not come naturally for organizations; it takes effort to build and create the type of collaboration that can create a positive atmosphere. We should not underestimate the difference this type of atmosphere can make in an organization. It should come as no surprise that *collaboration* is one of the 4Cs discussed in Chapter 2. The 21st century skills are necessary for all of us in the workforce today.

The third characteristic in our definition of school culture focuses on the ability of the school to **set goals** to improve and maintain school culture. Goal setting is often identified as a tool to help individuals achieve success. If goal setting is used in a team, corporate, or school setting, advancements within the group can be significant. We believe that this characteristic is also one that is often overlooked in the school setting. Chapter 5 is devoted solely to this topic.

The fourth characteristic centers on the school's ability to create an **action plan** for each goal through a **shared vision** and **strong communication**. Having a shared vision promotes cohesion and buy-in from the beginning of the action planning. Communication is a key attribute in any group dynamic and is central in building a strong organizational culture. As we have worked in many schools, we have found that communication is almost always one of the major issues in the school's culture. Too often, the lack of communication is not recognized and is an underlying issue that has a tremendous impact on every aspect of the school, especially the overall culture. Strong communication and a shared vision will provide support and will increase the probability of success for the action plan.

The fifth characteristic in defining a positive school culture is **assessing attitudes**. Attitude assessment includes a review of one's own attitude as well as a review of the attitudes of colleagues. Research shows that a positive attitude impacts the performance of individuals and organizations. In our coaching, our parent workshops, and many of our professional development programs for teachers, we focus heavily on the importance of positive attitude. The right attitude can put you in the right frame of mind to deal with daily issues. Sometimes the culture of our work environment does not encourage a positive attitude. When this is the case, we must take it upon ourselves to help foster a positive attitude in ourselves and our colleagues.

Engaging openness is the last characteristic in our definition of school culture. Engaging openness is an individual's willingness to try new things, provide input to the team, embrace change, and step out of his or her comfort zone. This characteristic pulls many of the other characteristics together.

The following list summarizes each of the characteristics from our definition of a positive school culture.

1. **Student Engagement:** Determine the engagement level of students in their personal learning and in the classroom.

2. **Collaborating to Determine and Prioritize Challenges and Opportunities:** Principals and teachers work as a team to voice positive and negative aspects of the school via interviews, surveys, and group activities.

3. **Set Goals:** Set goals to improve school culture.

4. **Action Planning:** Determine an action plan for each goal through shared vision and strong communication.

Creating a strong action plan for each established goal helps teams move forward with clarity and determination.

5. **Assessing Attitude:** Review your attitude and that of your colleagues.

6. **Engage Openness:** Determine your willingness to try new things, provide input on issues, embrace change, and step out of your comfort zone.

Focusing on these six characteristics helps move schools and our individual thinking from a 20th century learning culture to a 21st century learning culture that benefits everyone. As teachers embrace these six characteristics, they become empowered and assume the role of teacher–leaders in their schools. In the 21st century learning environment, teachers are truly the directors and leaders of their classrooms, and the six characteristics of school culture help shape teacher thinking. Using the discussion of Millennials and Gen I students in Chapter 1 and the definition of 21st century skills in Chapter 2, we have a clear idea of many of the concepts that need to be included in 21st century learning environments. We believe that a missing key component in education reform is creating school cultures that support 21st century teaching and learning. By actively focusing on each of the six characteristics in our definition, we can set the stage for successful 21st century learning. The overall school will have a more positive climate, teachers will feel

Teachers in a 21st century learning environment facilitate, instruct, collaborate and communicate with their students.

What Is School Culture and Why Is It So Important?

empowered, and the students will be more engaged with each other, their teachers, and their learning. In this environment, teachers facilitate, instruct, collaborate, and communicate with their students, taking the instructional leader concept to a new level in their classrooms.

Our focus in Chapter 3 on change also ties closely to creating a positive 21st century school culture. We believe that it is reasonable to argue that in the 20th century changes were not as significant in our society, and the impacts on education from a global perspective were not as great. Because we are well into the 21st century, it seems clear that many changes are necessary to provide the kind of learning opportunities we want for our children. The world is changing, and we must also change our schools and the cultures that they hold. This is a critical step in making our education system one that prepares students for the jobs and lives they will enjoy.

In our experience, school culture is an area that the entire staff rarely has a chance to focus on as a team. Whether a school wants to improve the working environment or the school knows it has lost its sense of community and family, taking the time to look at the overall culture is imperative in advancing the school. Small issues often keep organizations from working through challenges with a team approach to find solutions that are helpful and productive for everyone. As we have worked through cultural issues with schools, it is rewarding to see attitudes change as the issues around culture are addressed. The culture of the work and learning environment affects everyone involved, so it is critical that the school evaluate and set plans for improving culture for the sake of the students, teachers, staff, and principals.

The Effects of School Culture on Students

A school's culture sets the stage for **everything** that happens within the school. School culture affects every aspect of the school including academics, discipline, communication, and community and parent relationships. School culture also directly impacts the classroom and teacher. The teacher is ultimately in control of the classroom culture. Even schools with overall cultural challenges or known problems have individual classrooms with a positive culture. Students in these classrooms will likely tell you they like the teacher, they enjoy learning, and they feel safe and happy. Safety in terms of school does not mean just physically safe, but in a "safe space" where you feel safe to communicate and are free of judgment from teachers and peers.

The classroom culture then leads to students—their attitudes, their outlooks, their moods, their willingness to learn. The school and classroom culture determines whether the students have positive or negative *outlooks*, *opportunities*, and *achievement*. Outlook refers to the students' overall feelings about education—Do they feel empowered? Are they inspired? Are they supported and encouraged as they pursue opportunities both inside and outside the school? We realize that students may have negative behavior or attitudes based on factors that are out of your control. Individual students bring challenges, but we believe that you can have a positive impact on them and may be the only person who does. Even the most challenging students thrive in the right environment.

Students who would answer yes to the questions above are more likely to be offered and take advantage of *opportunities*. Examples of these may include such things as taking additional coursework, joining a traveling team, focusing on studying or choosing to go to college. These opportunities then lead to *achievement*— success in academics, and later in higher education and the workforce. Conversely, if the school and classroom culture is negative, then problems arise, apathy increases, and school systems begin to fail. A positive school culture creates better educational outcomes and student achievement.

Students who are exposed to positive school cultures take advantage of opportunities, have a positive outlook, and are more likely to achieve success in academics and extracurricular activities.

School Assessment

Improving school culture and attitudes begins with assessing what is working and what needs to be improved. A useful tool that we use in our *Who Took My Chalk?*™ program is the "Chalkboard of Challenges & Impacts." The chalkboard that follows is used as a reminder to us of the days of chalkboard and chalk. The chalkboard is the place where great knowledge was shared for many years. We use this classroom icon with the same philosophy, only this time asking teachers for personal challenges and impacts that they experience on a daily basis at their schools. Challenges are problems or issues that they face, and impacts are those things that can be most effectively addressed as a school team. Sharing this information helps to define the issues related to culture and ultimately to use them to build a more positive 21st century culture. This activity can provide you with a way to begin formalizing your thoughts around the current status of the culture of your school. Often, many of the major underlying issues in schools tie back to a variety of sometimes *unrelated* occurrences that change attitudes. It could be something as simple as a misinterpreted message that speaks to teachers in a negative way causing hard feelings and a switch in the teachers' attitude. It could also be something more direct, but either way, it is important to expose the issues.

Although little connection has been shown in the past between job satisfaction, job attitudes, and performance, a 1992 study by Cheri Ostroff looks closely at the relationship between employee satisfaction, other job-related attitudes, and organizational performance at the secondary school level. The study found, "Organizations with more satisfied employees tended to be more effective than organizations with less satisfied employees." We need satisfied employees in our schools to best educate our children. There is no greater place than in our schools where this job satisfaction should be evident. To create a 21st century positive school culture we must have —satisfied employees.

We will walk you through the steps of the "Chalkboard of Challenges & Impacts" activity and include an example of topics that surfaced when the teacher responses were combined at an overall school level. You will complete this activity on your own with your personal reflections and then, if your school chooses, summarize all comments for a school version.

Determine Where You Are—Assessing School Culture and Attitude

If a school adopts our definition of culture, it is important that each teacher and principal participate in the effort to assess school culture. This can occur in a number of ways. We recommend a survey that each teacher completes, such as the assessment that is reprinted on the next four pages.

Who Took My Chalk?™ Assessment Survey

Rank each question according to the 5-point Likert scale described below.

1 Low/Poor   2 Fair   3 Neutral   4 Good   5 High/Excellent

1. To what extent do you feel your students are responsible and accountable for their own learning in the classroom?

   ☐ 1   ☐ 2   ☐ 3   ☐ 4   ☐ 5

2. To what extent do you feel your students are active participants in their learning?

   ☐ 1   ☐ 2   ☐ 3   ☐ 4   ☐ 5

3. To what extent do you feel your students use 21st century tools as part of the classroom learning environment?

   ☐ 1   ☐ 2   ☐ 3   ☐ 4   ☐ 5

4. To what extent do you feel you make connections between your classroom instruction and the real world?

   ☐ 1   ☐ 2   ☐ 3   ☐ 4   ☐ 5

5. Rate the level of effective collaboration that leads to student achievement between teachers and administrators.

   ☐ 1   ☐ 2   ☐ 3   ☐ 4   ☐ 5

(continued)

Who Took My Chalk?™ Assessment Survey *continued*

6. Rate the level of effective collaboration among teachers that leads to improved student achievement.

   ☐ 1   ☐ 2   ☐ 3   ☐ 4   ☐ 5

7. Rate the level of effective structures in your school to provide time for teachers to work together.

   ☐ 1   ☐ 2   ☐ 3   ☐ 4   ☐ 5

8. To what extent has goal setting been effectively used to impact your school in a positive way?

   ☐ 1   ☐ 2   ☐ 3   ☐ 4   ☐ 5

9. To what extent do school leaders share responsibility with teachers to achieve school goals?

   ☐ 1   ☐ 2   ☐ 3   ☐ 4   ☐ 5

10. To what extent do you feel you have a voice in the decisions related to goals for your school?

    ☐ 1   ☐ 2   ☐ 3   ☐ 4   ☐ 5

11. How would you rate your school team's ability to identify necessary action to solve challenges?

    ☐ 1   ☐ 2   ☐ 3   ☐ 4   ☐ 5

12. How would you rate your confidence level in your school team to align the resources and staffing necessary to achieve specific goals?

☐ 1   ☐ 2   ☐ 3   ☐ 4   ☐ 5

13. How would you rate the level of opportunity you are given to share your expertise in creating and meeting action plans for your school?

☐ 1   ☐ 2   ☐ 3   ☐ 4   ☐ 5

14. How would you rate the attitudes of the teachers and staff at your school?

☐ 1   ☐ 2   ☐ 3   ☐ 4   ☐ 5

15. How would you rate your feelings when you walk into the school each day?

☐ 1   ☐ 2   ☐ 3   ☐ 4   ☐ 5

16. How important are attitudes in maintaining a strong school?

☐ 1   ☐ 2   ☐ 3   ☐ 4   ☐ 5

17. How would you rate your level of comfort with the rate of change taking place in your school?

☐ 1   ☐ 2   ☐ 3   ☐ 4   ☐ 5

(continued)

Who Took My Chalk?™ Assessment Survey *continued*

18. Rate your feelings about stepping out of your comfort zone.

    ☐ 1   ☐ 2   ☐ 3   ☐ 4   ☐ 5

19. Rate your feelings about overall communication at your school.

    ☐ 1   ☐ 2   ☐ 3   ☐ 4   ☐ 5

20. How would you rate the level of trust among teachers in your school?

    ☐ 1   ☐ 2   ☐ 3   ☐ 4   ☐ 5

21. How would you rate the level of trust among teachers and school administrators?

    ☐ 1   ☐ 2   ☐ 3   ☐ 4   ☐ 5

22. How would you rate the level of trust among teachers and students?

    ☐ 1   ☐ 2   ☐ 3   ☐ 4   ☐ 5

This survey asks teachers questions around the six school characteristics including the attitude of teachers, the engagement of students, openness to stepping out of one's comfort zone, how challenges are evaluated, and how goals and actions are set for achieving results. Reviewing the responses to the survey helps you understand the general school culture. For example, if many of the responses about trust within the school are negative, this could be one indicator of the overall culture.

If possible, one-on-one interviews should be completed with each teacher and administrator in your school. This face-to-face feedback is valuable to both collecting information and building a relationship with the staff. We suggest a third party (consultant or evaluator) for this to ensure individual privacy and unbiased discussions and reports. Not surprisingly, teachers are often concerned that they cannot share freely with district, school, or state representatives. This is not a negative reflection on any of these outside governing bodies, just a fact that prevents real issues from surfacing. If these issues do not surface, the school is rarely able to move forward. The education system and teachers end up with the same results and same negative cycles. A third party who has nothing to gain from the information is often more trusted and therefore provided with more detailed and truthful answers and information.

Analyze Results

Once all data have been collected, the findings are combined into a tool that we call the "Chalkboard of Challenges & Impacts." This board begins with a listing of all of the challenges from the surveys and interviews. Both teachers and administrators are often surprised to see what is really going on in the minds of their colleagues. This opportunity does however clear the air in a refreshing and encouraging way. From that point, goals are set and corresponding actions and responsibilities are created. This step in analyzing the culture is key in finding the underlying issues that affect school culture and hinder school progress. Without a strong team spirit and culture, it is difficult to move any organization forward. We have found the assessment work to be most effective in bringing key issues to the surface and allowing the school team to work through them. These are not always easy issues to talk about, but if left unaddressed, they continue to negatively impact the school culture and learning environment.

Figure 4.1 is a sample chalkboard from a school where we implemented *Who Took My Chalk?*™. All of the comments on the board were responses and feedback from face-to-face interviews with teachers. From this information, we worked with the teachers to determine the three most common challenges that could be positively affected and impacted by the group as a unified team. In this example, those were determined as (1) behavior and discipline, (2) communication, and (3) leadership and direction. It is interesting to note that this is an example from a real school as their top three challenges directly correlate to the results of our "Greatest Challenge" survey. These are key challenge areas in education that, when addressed, can make a significant difference in the school culture and student outcomes of the school. In this example, the school team used this information to set goals and take action to improve these challenge areas. The results were newly created discipline policies that everyone supported, improved methods of communication between and among teachers and administrators, and open and productive discussion about improvements that could be made in leadership strategies that resulted in a more productive work environment (see Figure 4.1).

Personal Assessment

Assessing attitudes is the process of personally looking at oneself and one's peers to become aware of issues surrounding positive and negative attitudes and the effects they have on

FIGURE 4.1 *Chalkboard of Challenges & Impacts*

Lack of cohesiveness/need to make clarification on who is in charge of what

Great faculty and team

Sit down and meet with each team—get to know us

Lots of staff support for each other

New teacher orientation

Better two-way communication

Positive reinforcement for staff is needed

Counselor as discipline—bad idea

Appreciate detailed, specific notes

Stress is high, so is work ethic

Resentment

More updates, more frequent

Use ISE days for training

What are priorities? Need that direction

Planning time is appreciated—Lunch and recess time

Go for excellence

Strong committees not being utilized

Frustrated because we can't meet all student needs

Follow through

Great leaders

Consistent rules across the board

Recognize hard work

Administrators need to visit classrooms—let students get to know administration

Feel like we're lacking direction

Need equity among all teachers

Administration needs to be more engaged with students

Excellent parent involvement

Impressive staff—proud to be here

Dedicated, intelligent teachers

Clear leadership

Lack clear definition

Set the example

Love the school

Too many things too fast

Change isn't the problem, it's how you go about it

Let presence be known

Teachers don't feel they have support

Lack of communication, when given fragmented, confusing, and partial

Lost message of intrinsic value

Impacts

1. Behavior/Discipline
2. Communication
3. Leadership/Direction

Who Took My Chalk?™

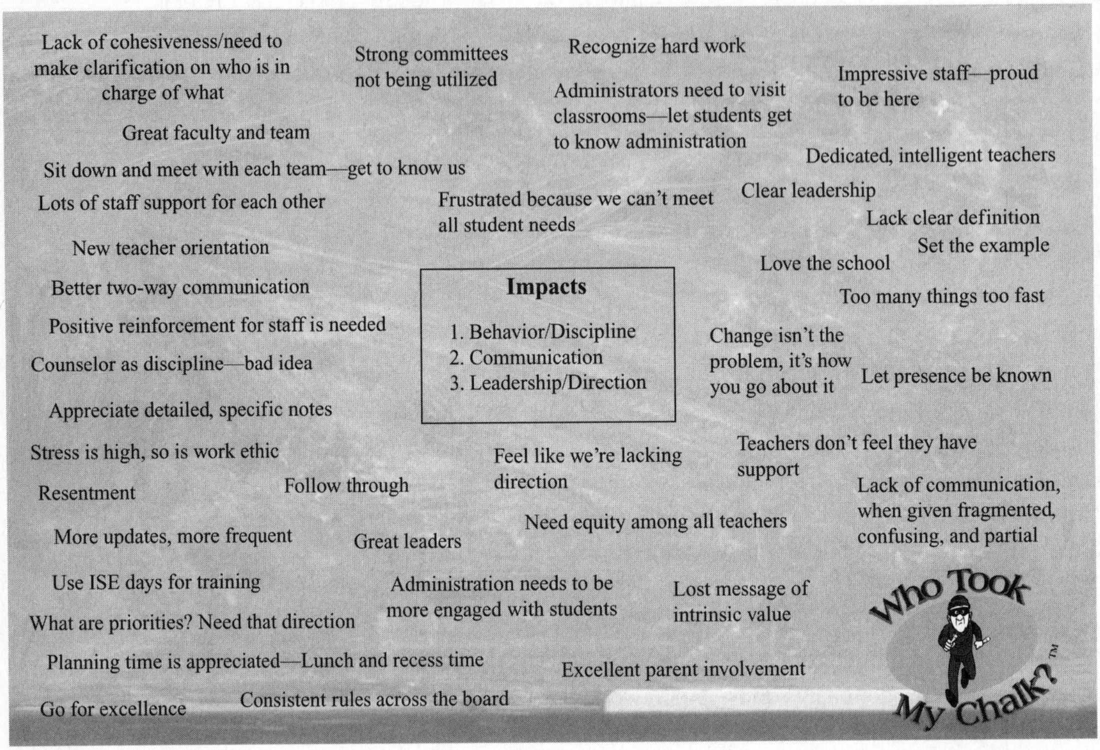

the school. A personal assessment is something that teachers rarely have the opportunity to do because of the demands on their time. Many in the business world attend workshops or coaching sessions that provide opportunities for personal reflection, but educators rarely have this opportunity. Experts in the field understand the importance and value of taking the time to look within, but daily life is often so demanding that teachers rarely have time to catch their breath, let alone spend time in personal reflection. As we reflect on the importance of the work that educators do, it is easy to see why we want those working with our children every day in our schools to have this opportunity.

Create Your Personal Chalkboard of Challenges & Impacts

We ask that you now take time to create your own "Chalkboard of Challenges & Impacts." Think about things that are concerning you about your school, your classroom, and your

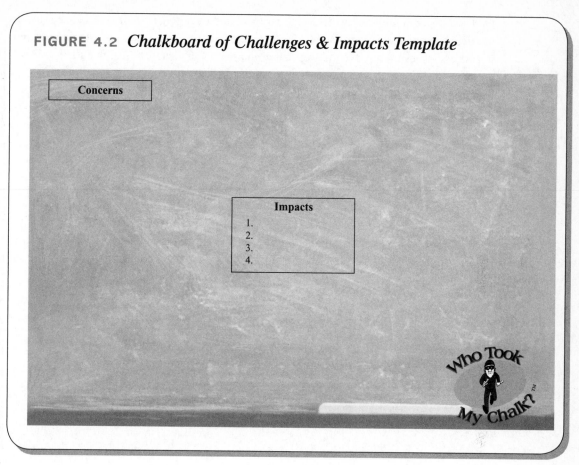

FIGURE 4.2 *Chalkboard of Challenges & Impacts Template*

teaching. What are the topics that instantly come to mind? What do you spend time talking about with your colleagues? What would you like to adjust in your school or your classroom?

At this point in the process, you need to be concerned only with the "challenges" section of the chalkboard (see Figure 4.2). Take time to brainstorm and include everything you can think of at this point. We will analyze and work through your thoughts in Chapter 5.

Chapter Summary

Twenty-first-century teaching and learning calls for a new school culture that supports students, teachers, and administrators in the learning process. Our definition of school culture focuses on six characteristics for schools—student engagement, collaboration, goal setting, action planning, assessing attitude, and engaging openness. Most schools do not dedicate enough time to focus on these characteristics or give teachers the opportunity to address issues to improve the work environment. Many teachers feel that their voices are never heard and that schoolwide communication around culture is rarely discussed because of the many demands and challenges that exist on a daily basis. The following reflections and activities will help reflect on the culture of your school and the culture you create in your classroom.

● Reflections

1. What does your school culture feel like? Is it positive, allowing students to have positive experiences, opportunities, and achievement? Is it negative, causing a block in creative, academic, and extracurricular opportunities? What areas could be improved?

2. How does your classroom fit into your overall school culture?

● Activities

1. Complete your personal "Chalkboard of Challenges and Impacts" (only the part described at the end of this chapter).

2. List the challenges you determined through this activity.

chapter 5

Set . . . and Achieve
Goals

Address Your "Chalkboard of Challenges & Impacts"

Now that you have created your "Chalkboard of Challenges & Impacts," it is time to take a closer look at the thoughts you generated and determine what they really mean. By doing so, you can determine how your energy is reflected in the contents. At this point, we are going to look at your list closely and from it create two separate lists—*Energy Wasters*

REACH GOAL!

STICK TO IT

GET TO WORK

MAKE PLAN

SET GOAL

and *Energy Savers*. This process will help you as you look at how you spend your time and how your time impacts the things you want to accomplish in your life. Most people set goals at some point in their lives—the difficulty is typically not in setting the goals, but in staying on track to meet those goals. As we think about teaching in the 21st century, it is easy to realize that, as we strive to adjust our instruction to meet the needs of today's students, we need to set and achieve goals to guide us through these evolving times. As we begin our journey of looking closely at ourselves and moving forward in the things that are important, let us begin by talking about the *Energy Wasters*.

Energy Wasters

Energy Wasters are things we worry about that are outside of our control. Often, we spend too much time and energy focusing on matters over which we have little or no control. In the school setting, this could include concerns such as new policies, changes in administration, or the pressures from outside influences on your school. For the purposes of this book, energy wasters are the things that are to a certain degree outside of your control. We are not saying that it is impossible to have an impact on a controversial policy or a questionable administrator with time and effort. In this case, however, we are referring to those issues that we do not plan to change ourselves. For these issues (or *Energy Wasters*), it becomes depleting to our own energy to talk, worry, or think negatively about them. This also relates back to our discussion of attitude in Chapter 3. Looking at your "Chalkboard of Challenges & Impacts," how many of the concerns you listed fall within this category? Put these concerns into their own list. A chart is provided at the end of this chapter to help you formalize your thinking.

Now look at your *Energy Wasters* list. Think about (and quantify, if you can) the amount of time you spend thinking about, talking about, or worrying about each item. Let's say you spend more than an hour per day on this list. During the school week, that is 5 hours you could be focusing on something positive that you *could* influence. Often, we get caught up in the thought that "there just isn't enough time" without actively looking at how we spend our time and where we can make adjustments if we really want to change. How can you change your thoughts and focus that energy on making real change in your own classroom? To do this, let's create your *Energy Savers* list.

Energy Savers

We call them *Energy Savers* because (1) worry and negative energy take more of your energy than positive energy; (2) by redirecting your energy to positive change, you will actually have more energy and be more motivated; and (3) our experience shows that many of the changes teachers want to make in their classrooms save them not only energy, but also time! Take some time to create your list of *Energy Savers* in the chart at the end of this chapter.

When choosing your energy savers, consider what is most important and what will make the biggest difference to you and your students.

Now looking at your list, prioritize the concerns in the order that you would like to address them. You may want to do this based on which ones concern you most and would therefore create the biggest impact if they were resolved. From this list you will develop your goals. For example, let's say one of your concerns is that you do not have time to make changes to your lesson plans. This is a concern that you can directly impact and, if changed, could make a huge difference in your students' level of engagement and ultimately, achievement. Another example might be that you are concerned about the lack of communication among the teachers at your school. Within a certain wing, teachers are connected, but throughout the school, there seems to be lack of communication between teachers. You know this is counterproductive to any new efforts you are trying to implement on a schoolwide basis. These are examples of concerns that could be framed as goals and addressed, either on your own or along with others in your building.

Now that you have looked objectively at your concerns, you have two lists giving you a clear picture of the things that are taking time and energy away from you and those you can influence. Now, take your *Energy Wasters* list, crumple it up, and throw it away. If you did it on the computer, delete it. Make a commitment to yourself to put those things behind you. When they creep back into your mind or conversations, remind yourself that your time is too valuable to waste on issues that do not create value in your life. Think back to the act of throwing away or deleting the old concerns. From this point forward, you will focus on the list of concerns that you can directly impact—your *Energy Savers*.

Address Your "Chalkboard of Challenges & Impacts"

Visualize the End Result

Before we start writing specific goals, we would like you to think about the big picture. In other words, what does success look like to you in a 21st century learning environment? Take some time to really think about this so that you are able to clearly define what it looks like for you to have the classroom and the outcomes you desire. What would your ideal day look like? These questions will help get you started as you conceptualize your ideal learning environment. Remember to answer these questions based on how you want the answers to be or how you want your life and classroom to look. The purpose of this exercise is to visualize what your ideal environment looks like after your goals are accomplished. You can answer these questions in the space provided at the end of this chapter.

Visualize Your Ideal Environment

1. How do you feel when you wake in the morning and look forward to your day?

2. What does your morning look like before you arrive at school?

3. In what kind of school do you teach? How are the environment and school culture?

4. What does your classroom or learning environment look like?

5. What kind of tools and resources are available to you to teach the way that you want to teach?

6. What is your role as the teacher?

7. How do your students interact with you? Each other?

8. How engaged are the students? What are the mood and feel of the environment?

9. How involved are the parents at your school and in what ways? How do they support you in your teaching?

10. What types of instruction do you use to teach your students?

11. What ultimate outcomes do you desire for your students?

12. How do you feel when you leave your school at the end of the day?

Set Your Goals

We begin this section by recognizing that teachers probably set more goals and objectives than any other professional. However, we ask that you reflect on the comments here and think about this goal setting in a different way than you have in the past for your lesson plans. Open your thinking to really embrace the ideas that we suggest for yourself personally and professionally. This probably feels a little unusual because we rarely take the time to do this type of exercise.

Goal setting is not a new concept in our society. Research continues to grow in this area, and it is interesting to look at how many successful people rely on this way of thinking. The resource bank is flooded with authors discussing goal setting and its importance in our lives. If we consider Thomas Edison as an example and think about his thousands of attempts before successfully inventing the light bulb, we can quickly see that staying focused on the goal was an important part of his accomplishment. This focus is sometimes lost in our schools by both our students and our teachers. In her article, "Goal Setting for Students and Teachers: Six Steps to Success (2005)," Laura A. Rader defines six steps for successful goal setting for students and teachers. The six steps are: choosing a specific goal and writing it down, determining an achievement time period, creating a plan of action, visualizing the accomplishment, working hard, and evaluating. These six steps work for teachers and students alike. Rader states that "successful people always have had clear, focused goals that guide them to greatness."

Napoleon Hill is well known for his book *Think and Grow Rich*, which was first published in 1937. Hill studied a number of famous, successful individuals for over

A Note on Personal Goals ● Although this book is written with a focus on teachers creating goals for their classrooms, it is important to take a holistic view. Our professional lives are impacted by our personal lives, and the opposite is also true. To create goals and move forward in your classroom, there may be aspects of your personal life that you want to improve as well. For example, if you are someone who has trouble getting organized at home, you may have that trouble in your classroom as well. It is easy to think that we can focus only on what happens in our classroom, but to truly create the learning environment you want, you may also have to set personal goals to help get you where you want to be on all levels of your life. Continuing with the example of being unorganized, if you have trouble getting to school on time because your morning routine is unorganized and chaotic, this unorganized start to your day can lead to the same environment in your classroom. In other words, sometimes when we get off to a rocky start in the morning, it is difficult to recover throughout the day. We point this out because it is so important to look at the big picture of our lives, including all the things that use our time and energy.

twenty years to create a list of steps one should follow to be successful. In these steps, he focused on creating an organized plan and on making decisions. Reflections on his work today indicate that his steps in personal development were really about goal setting. According to *Goal Achiever* (2001) by Bob Proctor, "Your goals should be something you want—not something that you need." As you begin to set your goals, remember to create goals that will make a difference in your life and be worth pursuing wholeheartedly.

Life is full of distractions. As you begin setting your goals, be sure that you truly focus on what is most important to you. Do not let the past get into your thinking or get in your way. You must look forward and think about where you want to be and how you want to get there. Dream big as you set your goals and base your goals on what you think you can do. Do not focus on *how* you will get there at this point. Dream big and design a future that puts you where you want to be. Consider this thought from Abraham Maslow, "If you plan on being anything less than you are capable of being, you will probably be unhappy all the days of your life."

SMART Goals

Now that you have a vision of what you ultimately desire for your classroom, look back at your *Energy Savers* with your vision in mind and begin creating goals that will give you a clear path to follow to success. The best way to set goals is to keep them simple and break them down into tangible parts so that you can see clearly what you need to do to move forward. Using the SMART Goal process will help ensure that you are setting goals that are within reasonable limits. Although it is difficult to pinpoint when the SMART Goal process originated, it is a widely used method for goal setting

Setting SMART Goals is a key component to success in any initiative.

. . . .

75

referenced by such noted authors as Zig Ziglar, Ken Blanchard, and Steven Covey. Also used by IPEC Coaching in the training of its coaches, it provides a clear and simple way to create goals.

SMART Goals

S	**Specific**	What do you want to achieve?
M	**Measurable**	How will you know when you reach it?
A	**Attainable**	Is it possible and worth striving for?
R	**Realistic**	What resources do you need? How will you do it?
T	**Time-Oriented**	By when will you achieve it?

Specific   A specific goal has a much greater chance of being accomplished than a general goal. To set a specific goal, you must answer five "W" questions:

- Who?:   Who is involved?
- What?:   What do I want to accomplish? Be specific.
- Where?: Where will the activity take place?
- When?:   When will the goal be accomplished?
- Why?:   Why am I doing this? What is the reason, purpose, or benefit of accomplishing the goal?

   EXAMPLE: A general goal would be "Create a wiki." But a specific goal would be "Create a science wiki for my students to exchange information about current lessons and post data they collect in the field."

Measurable   Establish concrete criteria for measuring progress toward the attainment of each goal you set. When you measure your progress, you stay on track, reach your target dates, and experience the exhilaration of achievement that spurs you on to continued effort required to reach your goal. To determine if your goal is measurable, ask questions such as these: How much? How many? How will I know when it is accomplished? Using the science wiki example, you would determine the grading period the wiki would be ready for use.

Attainable When you identify the goals most important to you, you begin to determine ways you can make them come true. You develop the attitudes, abilities, skills, and financial capacity to reach them. You begin seeing previously overlooked opportunities to bring yourself closer to the achievement of your goals.

You can attain most any goal you set when you plan your steps wisely and establish a time frame that allows you to carry out those steps. Goals that may have seemed far away and out of reach eventually move closer and become attainable. The art of goal setting is creating goals that are worthy of striving for, but not out of reach.

Realistic To be realistic, a goal must represent an objective toward which you are both *willing* and *able* to work. In the example of education, make sure that the skills and resources are available to you so that your goal is attainable. Create a plan to get there, making your goal realistic from where you are at the moment. For example, it may be more realistic to say that you are going to change three of your units to incorporate the 4Cs than to say that you will change your entire curriculum. Your goal is probably realistic if you truly *believe* that it can be accomplished. It also helps to ask yourself what conditions would have to exist to accomplish this goal. If the conditions that must be present seem unrealistic or completely out of reach, adjust your goals to make them more realistic.

Time-Oriented Set a time frame for the goal: by next week, within 3 months, by the end of the school year. Putting an end point on your goal gives you a clear target to work towards. If you do not set a time, the commitment is too vague. It tends not to happen because you feel you can start at any time. Without a time limit, there is no urgency to start taking action now.

By now, you may know exactly what goals you want to create. If so, great! If not, look at your *Energy Savers* list again. From this list, choose your top three and create a corresponding goal using the template above. Depending on the size of the goals, you can focus on them simultaneously or one at a time. The following is a list of sample goals for creating 21st century engaging learning environments and growing individually based on our discussion in Chapter 2.

Sample Goals for 21st Century Teaching and Learning

- Integrate technology and the 4Cs into one curriculum unit per semester.
- Build more collaborative student-teacher and student-student relationships in my classroom by incorporating three new ideas to get to know my students by the end of the first grading period.

It is important to put a time limit on your goals and also categorize short- and long-term goals for prioritization of the action steps that will follow.

- Transform my classroom into a more welcoming environment over the course of the semester using student creativity to design signage, electronic communication, and group activities for students and parents.

- Design more collaborative activities for my classroom by restructuring a lesson for every subject that I teach by the end of the December.

- Find and utilize three lessons that incorporate project-based learning by the end of the school year.

- Personally use critical thinking to restructure my schedule so that I have time daily to find learning opportunities and resources for use in my classroom every week.

- Focus on stepping out of my comfort zone to try two new activities per week in my classroom.

- Begin each class period with a word problem that students work in teams to solve.

- Modify my lesson plans by October to incorporate a weekly video that showcases the use of math skills in the workplace.

Differentiate Long-Term and Short-Term Goals

"The journey of a thousand miles begins with one step."

—Lao Tzu

For purposes of the education calendar, we determine long-term goals as those that span more than one school year. Short-term goals are those that can be accomplished within one school year. Depending on the scope and content of our goals, it may be helpful to list the long-term goals first, followed by the short-term goals. This will help you guide yourself as you create steps to reach each goal.

Using the goal chart at the end of this chapter, list each goal, and under the goal, create the corresponding steps it will take to achieve the goal. These steps will provide you with a clear chronological path to reach your goal. Start with the goal and work through the necessary steps from the largest to smallest. Using the steps, create a time line to help you map out the steps of the goal over the school year (or longer for the long-term goals).

Take Action

You have set your long- and short-term goals and created the steps that lead to achieving each goal. All of this is wasted without action. Commit yourself to this process and the work that you have already done by starting right now. Determine which goal you want to achieve first and begin following the steps that will lead you to success. Throughout this book, we will continue to provide you with strategies and tools that will help you succeed in creating exactly the classroom that you desire.

Achieve Your Goals

"In my mind, I'm already there!"

A discussion of goals would not be complete without talking about actually achieving them. Goals are best when they are achieved! The following ideas take goal setting to the next level so you are more likely to achieve them. Many of these ideas stem from Napoleon Hill's research. Through our training and coaching, we have found these practices to be effective time after time.

1. *Visualize the Outcome with Clarity*

We talked about visualizing the end result in the change process. Here, we just want to emphasize the *clarity* part of the idea. The clearer you are about every detail, the more your results will match that vision. You can also create a vision board as part of this process.

Vision Board Exercise Create a vision board of your ideal classroom environment by using a method that you are comfortable with. Design a poster board using traditional paper or try Glogster as a new tool for doing the same thing. Find pictures in old magazines, print pictures from the Internet, or even use real photos to construct a collage of the environment that you are creating. Use pictures of your children learning, materials or resources you would like in your classroom, and so forth. Have fun with this. If you are reading this book with peers, do this project together to motivate and inspire one another. Another option if you prefer to use only words is to place them into Wordle. Display your vision board in a place where you will see it regularly—in your classroom, your office, your bedroom, wherever you will see it several times a day. Note: You can also do this as a digital image that you create and use as the background on your computer desktop.

A Testament to Goal Setting ● In our company, we practice the group goal-setting approach. During an off-site meeting a few years ago, we worked with a facilitator to set not only goals for the organization, but also personal goals. Each of our employees stated a personal goal as we moved around the table. Three years later, as we look at those individuals, almost every goal that was stated out loud during our off-site meeting has been achieved. Some staff members were striving to be good parents and juggle the challenges of a working parent. Some had specific career goals in mind, while others discussed educational aspirations. As we reflect back today, we can see that almost every person has fulfilled his or her stated goal. Some moved on to complete their goals in schools or other organizations, while others are still moving ahead professionally with the organization. This is a testament to the goal-setting process and its effectiveness. We have seen it happen, and we know that it works.

2. *Write It Down and Be Committed.*

Written goals clarify your thinking and deepen your commitment. A common practice of successful people is keeping their written goals visible and reviewing them daily. We have seen it work countless times both with clients and in our own lives. By keeping a constant reference to what you are achieving and reaching for, you are always thinking in a positive direction. This also leaves less room and time for the *Energy Wasters* to creep back into your mind. Your commitment is the foundation for the outcome of your goals and will make the difference between success and "just another passing trend."

3. *Act, Live, and Speak as if It Is Already True.*

Regardless of how far away from your goals you feel, acting, living, and speaking as if they are already achieved will give you and the goals more energy and more motivational force. For example, instead of saying "I want my students to be engaged in my classroom," you should say "My students *are* engaged." This will create the mindset of success and positive thinking versus feeling like it is out of your reach. You are still working toward your specific goals, but the difference is you live as if they are already true.

Chapter Summary

As we think about teaching in the 21ˢᵗ century, it is easy to realize that, as we strive to adjust our instruction to meet the needs of today's students, we need to set and achieve goals to guide us through these evolving times. Use the reflections and activities in this chapter to determine your *Energy Wasters* and *Energy Savers* and create the goals that have resulted from your assessment. Follow the steps to achieve your goals and create the results you want in your classroom.

• Reflections

1. Assess your Chalkboard of Challenges and Impacts

   Using the discussion at the beginning of this chapter, list your *Energy Wasters* below, along with the estimated amount of time you spend on each per week.

Energy Wasters and Time Spent

Energy Wasters	Amount of Time Spent per Week
1.	
2.	
3.	
4.	
5.	

Using the description in this chapter, list your *Energy Savers* below.

Energy Savers

Energy Saver
1.
2.
3.
4.
5.

After you have determined your *Energy Savers*, prioritize them in the order you would like to address them. From this list you will develop your goals.

2. Visualize the End Result—Complete the visualization activity from this chapter by answering the questions below.

- How do you feel when you wake in the morning and look forward to your day?

- What does your morning look like before you arrive at school?

- In what kind of school do you teach? How are the environment and school culture?

- What does your classroom or learning environment look like?

- What kinds of tools and resources are available to you to teach the way that you want to teach?

- What is your role as the teacher?

- How do your students interact with you? Each other?

- How engaged are the students? What are the mood and feel of the environment?

- How involved are the parents at your school and in what ways? How do they support you in your teaching?

- What types of instruction do you use to teach your students?

- What ultimate outcomes do you desire for your students?

- How do you feel when you leave your school at the end of the day?

3. Set Goals

   Reflecting on your *Energy Savers* list and the visualization that you just completed, use the table at the top of the next page to list three to five goals you would like to accomplish as a school team. Under each goal, create the steps it will take to reach the destination. These steps will provide you with a clear chronological path to reach your goal. Start with the goal and work the steps down from largest to smallest. Using the steps, create a time line to help you map out the steps of the goal over the school year (or longer for the long-term goals). See the example below:

Goal-Setting Example

Goal

Integrate technology and the 4Cs into one curriculum unit per semester.

Action Needed	By When?	How will I do It?	✓
Determine units to modify	*End of next week*	*-look at units to determine which would lend best to the use of technology*	☐

4. Achieve Your Goals!

   Choose at least one of the success strategies under Goal Achieving and commit to it. Follow the steps described to take action today! Use the Goal-Setting Template to track progress and make adjustments as needed.

Goal-Setting Template

GOAL 1:			
Action Needed	**By When?**	**How will I do It?**	✓
			☐
			☐
			☐

GOAL 2:			
Action Needed	**By When?**	**How will I do It?**	✓
			☐
			☐
			☐

GOAL 3:			
Action Needed	**By When?**	**How will I do It?**	✓
			☐
			☐
			☐

GOAL 4:			
Action Needed	**By When?**	**How will I do It?**	✓
			☐
			☐
			☐

GOAL 5:			
Action Needed	**By When?**	**How will I do It?**	✓
			☐
			☐
			☐

Communicate Clearly

Communication is central to everything. In schools, communication (or lack thereof) can create a path to success (good communication) or be the cause of conflict and demise (bad or no communication). Of the many schools we have worked with through the *Who Took My Chalk?*™ program, a large percentage of them include communication as an

issue of concern on their Chalkboard of Challenges & Impacts. Communication then becomes the focus of corresponding goals for improvement in the school. The types of communication issues vary, but often start with the smallest things that can have a major impact on the overall school and on individuals. The lack of details in bulletins and e-mails, the timeliness of specifics for school field trips, and presentations from outside organizations that send the wrong message are all examples of poor communication in schools. No matter how big or small the issue, communication challenges make a difference in the overall operations of the school.

We often share one specific example involving an external agency presentation. In the presentation to teachers which was intended to discuss the roles of teachers and academic curriculum coaches, the coaches were referred to as "the experts." The teachers in the school who were working hard to meet Adequate Yearly Progress were offended by this reference to the coaches as the experts and it created turmoil in the school. The discontent grew and caused serious culture issues within the school. During the process of assessing the school through *Who Took My Chalk?*™, this problem surfaced, and we were able to work together to understand this issue. The coach who had given the presentation was unaware of the negative feelings it had created in the teachers. This may seem like a simple misunderstanding, but it grew into a problem that was causing tangible issues on a daily basis. With timely and appropriate communication, this challenge could have been dealt with quickly and easily.

As a step in our *Who Took My Chalk?*™ model, communication refers to modeling communication and collaboration for our students. As one of the 4Cs, communication is not only important for our students to learn as a skill, but also for us to model in our teaching and our professional relationships. For your purposes and the goals you set in Chapter 5, we devote this chapter to communication strategies that help you with peers, students, administrators, parents, and even your own children as you follow the necessary

Students who learn communication skills are able to express ideas easily, work in teams, and solve problems using a variety of communication tools.

●
....

88

steps to reach your goals. Regardless of your goals, communication is key to your success as you strive to improve or enhance relationships with students, peers, parents, and administrators.

Within a collaborative 21st century culture, teachers are modeling communication and collaboration skills. In the past, you may have seen yourself as a mentor to your students. In the 21st century context, you are becoming a coach and facilitator to your students. Many teachers referenced this indirectly in our "Greatest Challenge" survey when they discussed the many roles they assume in the classroom. Differentiating instruction, interacting with students and parents, and helping students work through social and emotional challenges call for teachers to be coaches and facilitators. Varying academic levels in our classrooms cause us to group and individualize instruction more than ever. Facilitating this type of instruction increases the need for multiple communication tools and skills in the classroom.

Aligning with the P21 framework, the skills that we provide in this chapter focus on (1) how to communicate effectively using specific communication and coaching tools and (2) ways to communicate with your students through a variety of communication tools. First, let's focus on coaching and communication tools.

Using Innovative Communication Skills to Coach and Facilitate

The tools that we share with you in this section can be used in your teaching as you communicate with students, peers, administrators, and parents. The P21 description of communication, discussed in Chapter 2, aligns with our suggestions for effective communication. Essential components of 21st century communication include the following:

- Articulate thoughts and ideas effectively using oral, written, and nonverbal communication skills in a variety of forms and contexts
- Listen effectively to decipher meaning, including knowledge, values, attitudes, and intentions
- Use communication for a range of purposes (e.g., to inform, instruct, motivate, and persuade)

Some of these tools may be familiar to you. In that case, they may serve as reminders to help you through the difficult situations that you face daily. Although reading about communication tools is not the best way to learn them, we thought it was important that this book include tools that you can immediately utilize. Practice is key, for you will improve your ability to quickly and easily use the tools by practicing them regularly. The following skills represent our experience-based modifications to coaching skills taught by the Institute for Professional Excellence in Coaching (www. iPECcoaching.com) and referenced in *Co-Active Coaching* (Whitworth, Kimsey-House, & Sandahl, 1998). We have modified these tools specifically for teachers, based on what you may encounter in your daily work.

Tool #1. Focused Listening

Listening is the foundation for effective communication. Effective and focused listening can increase the value of conversations and decrease frustration and wasted time. Although focused listening is not a new idea, we do not often use it in basic conversation. It is a way of listening and responding to another person that improves mutual understanding. Often, when people are in general conversation with one another, they do not actively listen. Rather, they relate what they hear back to their own life. Focused listening is a structured form of listening and responding that focuses the attention on the *speaker*.

When we practice *focused listening*, these are some of the questions we can answer:

- What is this person trying to tell me?
- What is this person's response style to change?
- What matters most to this person?
- What is really going on in this situation?
- Are this person's words and actions aligned?
- What is *not* being said?
- What motivates or inspires this person?
- How does the person handle conflict?
- How does the person respond to various situations?
- How does the person handle change?

Consider the difference between *conversational* or *"me"* listening and *focused* listening in the examples below:

> *"Me" Listening* This is the type of listening that takes place in most conversations. The listener is focused on her/himself, hence the term "me" listening. "Me" listening is also referred to as Level I or internal listening because the listener is more internally focused than focused on the speaker (Whitworth, Kimsey-House, & Sandahl, 1998). The speaker does not often

feel heard or understood because the listener is thinking about a response. Think about being at a party when someone is telling a story about a humorous thing that happened. Everyone who is listening thinks about a story in his own life, and then tells that story. During the speaker's story, listeners are focused more on the story they are waiting to tell, than on the speaker. We are not trying to say that "me" listening is in bad taste; in fact, it is just basic conversation. The following are two examples.

Teacher   *I really had a difficult time rewriting my lessons to incorporate technology.*

Peer as "Me" Listener   *"I know what you mean. It took me forever just to create one new unit on* Hamlet.*"*

– – – – – – – – – – – –

Student   *It took me all night to finish this homework assignment. It was really long.*

Teacher as "Me" Listener   *"Wait until you are in college. I spent many long nights on assignments then."*

Put yourself in the shoes of the listener in both examples. Nothing negative or wrong was said, but how satisfied do you think the listener feels?

Focused Listening   Focused listening means listening to the speaker and what he is saying, without thinking about what the speaker is saying means to you. The listening is focused on how the speaker feels and what is really going on with what he is saying and even what he isn't saying, but expressing through emotion and nonverbal communication.

Teacher   *I really had a difficult time rewriting my lessons to incorporate technology.*

Peer as Focused Listener   *I know this was a huge undertaking. You really put a lot of work into it, and I know it will pay off for you. Great work!*

– – – – – – – – – – – –

Student   *"It took me all night to finish this homework assignment. It was really long."*

Teacher   *"It sounds like you really focused and put a lot into the assignment. That shows that you care about your work."*

It is easy to practice this as long as you have conversations with other people! Notice the way that you listen in your next conversation. What are you thinking about? Many times, we are thinking about what we are going to say next. We have found that by listening actively, you actually have to say *less*, because you listen and get it right the first time. Often, people really just want to be heard.

Tool #2. Clarifying

Communication is heightened and much more effective when all parties involved feel that they have been heard and understood. Think about this from your own perspective. When you have spoken to a group, whether it is your peers or your students, how did it feel when you knew they were listening? And when you actually heard or saw the evidence that they "got it"? This leads to a good feeling as a teacher, knowing that your students are hearing and understanding what you teach. On a personal level, think about how it feels when you are speaking with a friend or spouse and you really need to explain something.

A Note on Conflict and Listening ● When people are engaged in a disagreement or argument, they are often busy formulating a response to what is being said rather than listening to the other person. They assume that they know what the person is saying, and rather than pay attention, they focus on how they can respond with their opinions and get the last word. When in conflict, people often contradict one another, denying the other person's description of a situation. This tends to make people defensive, and they will either lash out, or withdraw and say nothing. However, if they feel that their opponent is actively listening to their concerns and cares about what they are saying, they are likely to explain in detail what they feel and why. If both parties involved in the conflict do this, the chance of being able to develop a solution to their disagreement becomes much greater.

Does it feel good when you know that the person hears and understands what you are saying? Clarifying is summarizing or paraphrasing what someone has said. By doing this, the speakers can verify whether we really understood what they are trying to tell us. Sometimes, this tool alone can relieve stress and tension, which is really useful in a work setting where change is occurring or when talking to students who feel frustrated or misunderstood. To clarify what someone is saying, reflect on what the person said in an authentic way, as in the following examples.

> **Teacher** *"I have been working on my website for months, and I just can't get to a point where I am happy with it."*

Peer   *"You are saying that you feel like it should be great by now with all of the time that you put into it?"*

– – – – – – – – – – – – – –

Student   *"I keep trying and trying to get my math grades up, but it seems that whatever I do, I just mess up on my tests."*

Teacher   *"It sounds like you are not happy with the results you are getting given how much you studied."*

Here are some ways that you can clarify what is being said to you.

- What I think you are saying is …
- In other words, you are saying …
- Let me see if I understand …
- Let me see if this is correct …
- Please tell me if I have understood correctly …
- Based on what you have said …

Remember that you may not always get it right when you clarify.

● **Jill**

"I use this tool to make sure that I am understanding my clients. There are many times when I clarify something a client has told me, and he/she helps me understand exactly what was meant by correcting parts of my summary. This is valuable to me as it helps me understand when I have made an assumption or just misunderstood. This also helps my clients clearly understand themselves since they have to think about what they are saying and sometimes look at it from someone else's perspective."

Practice this skill so you can make clarification a natural part of your conversation, based on what sounds the best to you. For example, you can just say what you hear by starting with "So…". This skill is valuable for venting students or peers who need to get something off of their chest. They need to feel that they have been heard so they can move forward.

Tool #3. Validating Emotions

Validating emotions is a tool that we have found to be most powerful when used correctly. Validating comes after we have clarified what someone has said, because it is important that we clearly understood what that person was trying to say. When we validate individuals, we let them know that it is okay for them to feel the way they do and perhaps even normal, depending on the situation. Validating emotions works well when someone is upset or frustrated. Consider the following examples:

Teacher   *"I am really frustrated that my computers always have some kind of problems."*

Peer   *"That's understandable. It is frustrating when you are trying to use something to make things easier and it isn't working correctly."*

– – – – – – – – – – – – –

Student   *"I'm really upset that I didn't get an A on my paper."*

Teacher   *"I can see how this would be upsetting. You spent a lot of time working on that paper."*

In this example, you aren't saying that you should have given the student a better grade; you are merely saying you understand that the student is upset. You could follow this statement with feedback about the paper to explain the grade, if necessary. Sometimes when you validate a person, you can hear the relief coming from him. Too many times in conversation, when someone is venting strong emotion, the listener says "I know how you feel." That is not validating. In fact, it is usually frustrating to the speaker who thinks that no one knows how he feels. In fact, even if we have been through the same situation as someone else, we don't know how that person feels. We are all different people, viewing the world through our own individual filters.

Here are some ways that you can validate emotions:

- I can understand why you are frustrated because …

- You feel that what happened to you is not fair. You have every right to feel hurt and angry.

- What you are explaining is a difficult situation. Anyone would feel overwhelmed in your situation.

- What you are feeling is normal. It can be very stressful dealing with difficult people.

- Given your feelings about _____, it is perfectly normal that you feel sad about what happened.

Use the examples above and find the language that works best with your personality and communication style. The value in mastering this skill is that these individuals release negative emotions, so they are able to move forward to a solution. Finally, remember that you are not saying that their opinion is right; rather, you are saying that they are entitled to their emotions. Once the negativity is released, then you can deal with the issue at hand.

To understand how powerful validating can be, think about the following.

> ● **Jill**
>
> *"I remember a conversation I was having with a close friend about change she was experiencing in her life. She is a Type A personality and always runs her life like a tight ship. At the time I was talking to her, she was feeling down because she felt stressed about the responsibilities she was bearing. I said to her, 'You are moving across the county, changing jobs, selling a house, buying a house and your husband is working out of the country while you do all of this. It is understandable that you are a little stressed.' There was a long pause on the phone and I could hear her exhale and release a lot of pent up emotions. 'Thank you!' she said. 'I needed to hear that.'"*

She just needed someone to tell her that it was okay for her to feel stressed. Without stepping back and seeing all that she was doing, she was looking at her feelings of stress as a weakness. Validating her emotions allowed her to release some of the anxiety so that she could recognize all that she was doing and move forward knowing that it would all get done and everything would be fine.

Tool #4. Powerful Questions

Using the right questions can get you through almost any situation. When we ask powerful, thought-provoking, or *empowering* questions, rather than disempowering or closed-ended questions, we open the door to creativity, intuition, and solutions. Powerful questions "invite introspection, present additional solutions and lead to greater curiosity and insight" (Whitworth, Kimsey-House, & Sandahl, 1998). In the school setting, powerful questions can invite our students to look inside, be creative, and find their own answers. The same can be said of teachers and administrators. Examples of powerful questions include the following:

- How could our school be transformed if we accomplish …?
- Who is doing what we want to do that we can learn from? How can we learn from them?
- What do you do best?
- How can you learn from this challenge to improve your future?
- How can we turn this (challenge) around?
- How can we have fun while we go through this process?
- What kinds of activities make you the most excited about learning?
- What are you most interested in learning?
- How do you learn best?
- How can we add value to the lives of our students?
- How does that (activity or behavior) serve you?
- What do you hope to achieve by the end of the year?
- What is the thing that we do best as a team?
- What strengths can we pull to get us through this challenge?
- What do I want to be known for as a teacher?
- How can we get the resources that we need?
- What would make this _____ better for you?
- Who do we know that can help us?

Tool #5. Bottom Lining

We all want to learn how to stop someone from rambling, how to save time, and how to move forward. Sometimes as listeners, we have to help others get to the point of the matter. Bottom lining is not meant to be offensive. It is done by finding a way to help the speaker stay focused, think about what is really going on, and move forward. Sometimes we do not have time to listen to a long story or extra details, even if we are interested in what the person is saying. This is especially true in the school setting with many students to teach and many demands on our time. Consider the following examples:

Teacher   *"I really had good intentions about meeting my 21ˢᵗ century goals this month, but then I got all of this extra work at school and I was even working at home at night, and that took me away from my family, and it just got away from me."*

Peer   **"What are you really trying say here?"**

Teacher   *"I didn't focus on any of my goals this month."*

Peer   *"What do you need to do to get focused?"*

Teacher   *"I need to keep them somewhere where I can see them throughout the day so they don't get put on the back burner."*

Peer   *"Then maybe I could help you come up with a plan for doing that now."*

— — — — — — — — — — — —

Student   *"I didn't bring back the laptop that I checked out for my math assignment. I was running late and my mom was telling me to hurry up and then the bus came early. I almost missed it!"*

Teacher   **"So what is really going on here?"**

Student   *"I forgot the laptop."*

Teacher   *"What do you need to do to remember it tomorrow?"*

Student   *"I could put it next to the door so I can grab it as I go out to catch the bus."*

Teacher   *"So how will you remember to do that?"*

Bottom lining is in the second line in the examples above (in bold). Based on the speaker's response to the bottom line question, the conversation then takes its own direction. Another way to help move someone forward is to ask, "What do you think is really going on?" This can be especially useful if a person is confused or is repeating the same thoughts over and over again. Asking this question stops the repetitive cycle and opens the person to the answer to the question, which will ultimately move the person forward.

Tool #6. Breaking Resistance

Resistance is common in any major change process. This is important to keep in mind, as it will also help you be prepared for these situations. Sometimes challenges do not appear as difficult if we can anticipate them. The biggest factor in determining how to break through resistance is understanding the cause of it. When we merely hit an obstacle in the road, it is often easier to find solutions than it is when the resistance is rooted in conflict or strong emotion. Either way, the following questions can help during those times when you feel resistance from someone you are speaking with who is experiencing a period of resistance. This is especially helpful with students, for resistance is common in the education environment.

- What is causing you to shut down?
- What bothers you about ...?
- What do you think is blocking you?
- What is really going on here?
- How would it feel to defeat this (fear/challenge)?
- How can you break through this obstacle?
- How else can we get this done?
- How can I support you in getting through this?
- What will it take to move you forward?
- How else can you look at this ...?

Determine How to Best Use Communication Skills

Now that you have reviewed (and practiced) these communication skills, think about when and where you could best use them as you pursue your goals. Think about specific situations where these skills could be applied, referring to Figure 6.1 for examples. This table lists situations or emotions that you may encounter as a teacher and then pairs with them a skill or skills that could be used to alleviate the situation. We know that communication with students is important and can pave the way for learning, but where else might these tools benefit you? Do you have a specific issue that you need to discuss

FIGURE 6.1 *Tools to Use with Specific Emotions or Situations*

Emotion or Situations	Tools to Use	Example Questions
Anger/Conflict	Focused Listening Clarify Validate Emotions	*It's understandable that you are feeling angry based on ___. How can I help you get through this?*
Resistance	Focused Listening Breaking Resistance	*How have you overcome challenges like this in the past?* *What would it take for you to feel differently?*
Shut Down	Powerful Questions	*What will it take to move you forward?*
Stress/Overwhelm	Powerful Questions	*What will make this easier?*
Negative Attitude	Focused Listening Clarifying Validate Emotions Powerful Questions	*What if you looked at this in another way?* *How could this benefit you?*
Confusion	Focused Listening Powerful Questions Bottom Lining	*What do you think is really going on?*
Rambling	Bottom Lining Clarifying	*What are you really trying to say?*

with your administrator(s)? Do you have an unresolved conflict with a peer teacher? Is there general tension or miscommunication between you and a peer or student? Think about how you can use these skills to alleviate the tension and wasted energy that negative communication can cause. Try these techniques. The person(s) with whom you are communicating probably won't notice that you are using the skills, but you will notice a difference in the outcome of your communication.

Although Figure 6.1 reflects the more difficult situations, you should not overlook opportunities to use the communication tools described in positive situations with students, peers, administrators, and parents. It is important to let people know specifically when they have done something positive. During these times, use specific examples and cite the strengths of the individual. People do not often focus on (or even notice) their own strengths. It can be valuable for you to help people see these strengths. This not only will show that you notice and appreciate them, but also may motivate them to do more. Further, taking ownership of their strengths can lead them to feel better about themselves and continue to move forward in the effort.

Remember that practice is critical to using these tools most effectively. Use these tools often and adapt them to your own style. You may even want to keep a cheat sheet in your classroom or nearby to remind you to use the tools when you need them. We promise that with continued use, you will see a big difference in the way you communicate and the results you are getting from your students and peers.

Utilize Multiple Media and Technologies

We have provided you with coaching skills as a tool for communicating more effectively with your students, peers, and administrators. Another component to the P21 description of communication is the ability to utilize multiple media and technologies and also to determine their effectiveness and assess their impact. How do we do this in our classrooms?

Students will be expected to utilize many types of communication in their lifetimes, some of which we can't even imagine today. Throughout the book, we discuss many ways that students communicate. As teachers, we should teach how to utilize these tools effectively and the protocol for using them. We can use some of the following methods of communication:

- Verbal presentations to groups
- Presentations using presentation software such as PowerPoint or Prezi
- Online video conferencing such as Skype or ooVoo
- Written digital communication—e-mail, texting, chatting
- Social networks
- Wikis and blogs

Utilizing many types of media and communication tools in the classroom provides students multiple modes of learning and also helps them apply communication skills in all areas of life.

Integrating these 21st century communication tools into your curriculum, where appropriate, allows you to teach students how to use these tools effectively and responsibly. Although many students use these tools informally with friends, it is important for them to learn the difference between personal, educational, and professional use. For example, speaking with a friend through video chatting looks very different from conducting a video conference with another class or student from a school in another state or country. Texting or tweeting with friends is very different from sending an e-mail message to a teacher or employer. These are communication skills that are not being formally taught in many cases and perhaps even overlooked. Too often, we assume that because the younger generations were born into technology, they know how to effectively use it and do not need instruction or guidance. The guidance is needed not in the use of the technology, but in the ways that these tools can be used to communicate effectively.

Chapter Summary

Most educators chose their profession because they feel or felt that they could make a difference in the lives of children, and ultimately, in the future of our society. Communication is central to everything. In schools, communication (or lack thereof) can create a path to success (good communication) or be the cause of conflict and demise (bad or no communication). Using coaching skills with students, peers, and administrators can help create better communication in our schools. Teaching students about how to use communication tools effectively is also a key component to embracing *communication* as one of the 4Cs in our schools.

• Reflections

To answer questions 1 and 2, choose one of the coaching skills discussed and integrate it into your conversations for one day.

1. What did you notice about infusing the skill into your daily interactions?

2. What experiences resulted from using the skill that may not have occurred had you not used the skill?

3. How can you integrate 21st century communication tools into your curriculum?

4. What type of protocol or etiquette do you think is important for our students to understand with respect to 21st century communication tools?

chapter 7

Predict Possible *Roadblocks*

At this point in the change process, it is important to think about what could stop you from achieving your goals. What could get in the way of your end result? By thinking about what might be barriers to your success, you can plan ahead so you will have strategies to meet them. Many of the common challenges that surfaced in our "Greatest Challenge" survey also serve as common barriers to change in education. We will look at some of those in depth in this chapter. As you read, think about your goals and what barriers may serve as obstacles to you in your process.

Common Barriers to Change in Education

In the process of any change initiative, common barriers arise that serve as obstacles to our progress. Although each of us is unique in the goals we have set for our specific schools and classrooms, common barriers surface in schools when large-scale change is taking place. We have found the most common barriers to change in education to be the following:

- Fear
- Events of the Past (Assumptions)
- Attitudes and Limiting Beliefs
- Resources and Time
- Self-Sabotage

Let's take a closer look at each of these.

Fear

As new events threaten the status quo and old ways of thinking, fear of change is common. When we feel threatened, we feel fear, which affects us both physically and emotionally. Fear can present itself in many forms in the school setting: What if I fail? What if this doesn't work? I don't want to change the way I do things. I like things the way they are now. Peter Senge, director of the Center for Organizational Learning at the MIT Sloan School of Management, is known for saying, "People don't resist change. They resist being changed." This is especially true in education when teachers feel that change is being forced on them. In our view of change through the *Who Took My Chalk?* ™ model, we hope that you will embrace change as something that YOU choose for yourself, your students, and your classroom. Feeling empowered about change helps alleviate some of the fear involved with change. Fear also presents itself in the other barriers to change, as an underlying element that creates resistance.

Events of the Past

Events of the past serve as barriers to education in two ways: (1) Events that were not successful produce the prediction that the same thing will happen again, and (2) it is easy to get stuck in the events or ways of the past. The following is an explanation for both statements.

It is easy to feel frustrated when you are asked to start a new program or initiative if you feel like similar programs in the past have not worked. It is important to not project negative results of the past onto new initiatives in your life.

In the first statement, the introduction of a new program or idea is sometimes met with resistance based on something that did not work before. Education has been home to many passing trends, so it can be difficult to get buy-in when introducing a concept, program, or policy. The category of "red tape" also aligns with this because teachers express concerns about policymakers making wide, sweeping changes in education. To overcome this barrier, it is important to recognize if you are associating the change—in this case, creating 21ˢᵗ century learning environments—with an event or change in the past. If you recognize that you are making this association, you can let it go and replace the negative associations with positive thoughts and strategies to help you meet your goals. When we predict that something will turn out the same way as it did before, we focus on the fear rather than on the possibility of success. If we replace this with a positive focus on our goals, we entertain success rather than failure.

Examples:

Education trends come and go. We have had big ideas in the past, and we did not follow through. How will this time be any different?

The last time we got new technology, half of it was never used.

The last time I tried something new in my classroom, my students did not perform better.

It seems like every time I try to be agreeable and go along with the group, the project never lasts, and I feel like I wasted my time and energy.

These associations and resulting negative thoughts create resistance in us and impede our ability to focus on our goals. When we think about this in the context of 21ˢᵗ century teaching and learning, it is important to remember why we are making these changes. The framework that we discuss and the changes that are needed are brought about by old ways of thinking and teaching to which our students do not relate. How can you overcome associating this movement with education trends of the past? One way is to look to your students. Are they engaged? Are they thriving and ready for the 21st century workforce? If not, it's time to embrace change and focus on the goals you have set for 21st century teaching and learning in your classroom.

The second way events of the past serve as barriers to change is by holding onto the mindset that things should be done the way they have always been done. Some aspects of education have looked the same for a very long time. The idea of a teacher standing at the front of a room, while students sit in rows and listen, is still ingrained in our view of a learning environment. These old ways of thinking are part of the reason that education reform is so difficult. Years of following the same procedures and teaching students the same way creates a comfort zone for many teachers. Stepping out of this comfort zone can be difficult, as we have discussed, but it is necessary for the sake of our students and for the future of our society. It is natural and habitual to follow routines of the past. By consciously making the effort to focus on successful completion of your goals. you can overcome this barrier to change.

Attitudes and Limiting Beliefs

We devoted an entire chapter to attitude and school culture because our work has shown us that these components should be at the beginning and the core of any change process. Negative attitudes and limiting beliefs hold us back from achieving our goals and creating positive change in our lives. Think about the following statements and whether you have ever thought or made them:

- *We are doing this only because it is a requirement.*
- *This process is not necessary.*
- *These changes will not make a difference.*
- *If I do this right, I will just be asked to do more.*
- *If I act like I am interested, I will be given more work to do.*
- *My school will never have the funds to buy the new technology tools that we want.*
- *Our school will never look like that.*
- *Professional development is a waste of time.*

These statements reflect negative attitudes and limiting beliefs. Limiting beliefs impede our ability to achieve the goals we have set. Over time, we may not even notice our limiting beliefs or our negative attitude because we have repeated the same story for so long that we actually believe it to be true. Think about your attitude as it surrounds your goals. Do you feel confident that you can achieve them, or are there thoughts that are causing resistance? Ask yourself: *How does believing in this idea affect me? Does it help me succeed or does it hinder me, and how?*

Sometimes, we realize that these negative thoughts or limiting beliefs are just old ways of thinking that do not serve us anymore. These are not so difficult to change. Other times, a limiting belief is ingrained in our way of thinking and takes time to reprogram. If this is the case for you, either try replacing the beliefs with new, positive affirmations that you can refer to often in your day, or come up with solutions to the limiting belief. For example, if you believe your school "will never have the funds to buy the new technology that you want for your science unit," create a list of ways that the funds could be obtained. This keeps your focus on the possibilities, provides you with real avenues to seek the funding, and replaces the old negative limiting belief. How could that belief be true when you have a list of many ways that it could happen? We realize that this is not always easy to do, but we have found that focusing on the positive creates a better mindset.

Resources and Time

Resources and time, or lack thereof, are two of the most common challenges that teachers face, according to our "Greatest Challenge" survey. In terms of goal setting and barriers to creating the change we want, we have to look at how we can make the most of the resources we have, find ways to get the resources we want, and create time to follow through with our goals.

Many schools do not have the funding and resources they need or want to do everything they would like to do. We have seen, however, that teachers are wonderfully creative professionals, who use what they have skillfully and make the most of all of their resources for students. If you need resources to help you reach the goals you set in Chapter 5, think about ways to get them and then take action. Be creative and think out of the box. It can be fun.

Lydotta

"Many years ago when I was teaching high school, a group of teachers and I decided that we needed to have a multimedia workstation for our students. The funding was not available from the school or district. As a solution, we held a "Dance for Technology" for adults with live entertainment donated by a wonderful community member. The dance was so well attended we actually held it three more times. We raised enough money to get our machine and many other tools that complemented our efforts. This might not work for you, but it was something that I had never considered as a school fundraiser until I tried it."

It takes time and focus to reach goals, especially when it comes to changing the way we teach. You may have your classroom routine down to a science, knowing what you will teach when and how because you have taught the same grade or subject for years. The thought of taking time to redo lesson plans and restructure your routines can seem daunting. No matter how strict or flexible your teaching routine, as a teacher, you may still face time as a barrier because of the many roles you play and the many demands on your time. Use this opportunity to really look at your days. How can you find time to focus on the goals you have set for yourself? Where can you make adjustments that serve you and your students? Where can you say no?

One of the common things we hear from teachers and life coaching clients is that there does not seem to be enough time to fit everything that we want into our lives. We ask you—how often do you say "no"? Too often, we say "yes" to everything that is asked of us, without considering that we are actually saying "No!" to something else. If we say "yes" to taking an extra project after school, we may be saying "no" to time that could be spent working toward our goals. Consider this. Every time you say "yes" to one request, you are saying "no" to something else. We realize that finding the perfect balance is difficult, but just being aware of this concept can change how you look at requests on your time. How can this help you create more time to focus on change for your classroom?

Self-Sabotage

Self-sabotage is the negative self-talk that plays in our heads to remind us of why we can't accomplish something. It is the voice in our head that resists change or keeps us from reaching our goals. This negativity stems from fear and the desire to protect ourselves from the unknowns that change can bring to our lives.

Examples:

- *I can't do it.*
- *I'm not capable of learning how to use new technology.*
- *I'm not as technical as other people.*
- *I've never been creative.*
- *I'll never be able to re-create my lessons using problem-based learning.*

It takes time to overcome self-sabotage, especially for those who hear it the loudest and most often. If you see this in yourself, make note of the messages you are sending yourself. Replace those thoughts with positive thoughts that affirm your ability to meet your goals. This takes time and practice, but it does quiet the voices over time. Remember that the voice is there to protect you from stepping out of your comfort zone into the unknown—even if the unknown is positive. It is also important to note when self-sabotage occurs and then to use that knowledge to minimize or silence the voices. For example, do you hear the self-sabotaging voices when you are tired? When you are around certain people? When you are trying something new?

● Jill

"Over time, I have noticed that my own self-sabotaging voices come out at times when I am tired and still have a lot to do. I begin feeling overwhelmed as I think 'I can't get it all done' or 'I'm not happy with how much I got accomplished today.' When I take a moment to stop and realize what is happening, I acknowledge that I am tired and I go to bed. The next day, the voices are gone and I am ready to go again."

If you can pinpoint when the voices are loudest, you can find ways around them or learn to avoid them altogether.

Response Styles to Change

The barriers we discussed manifest themselves in response styles to change—a set of common behaviors and attitudes that one exhibits in the face of change. We have developed four "characters" depicting the four most common response styles to change we see in education. The following is not meant to categorize you or your peers; rather, it is intended to help you understand how you may be responding to change and what barriers are contributing to that response style. Within each description are suggestions to help you if you fall into that category and suggestions to help you work with each type as you implement change in your classroom. Sometimes it is the response styles of others impeding your work. For example, you may be dealing with resistance from peers or your principal as you try new ideas or make changes in your classroom. In that case, you can use the suggestions following each response style, along with the coaching skills in Chapter 6, to help you work with those people.

The Resistor

Resistors are the last to change, if they change at all. They really dislike change and often make it difficult for a team to move forward. The resistor's response to change is inevitably, "I hate it!" Consider Jane, the school librarian for 20 years.

Jane is in her early fifties. Although she could retire soon, that is not her main focus. She loves her job. She loves it so much that she doesn't want it or anything about it to change. You would not really know that Jane loves her job, because what she loves most is complaining and making a tightly run ship out of her library. So you shouldn't be surprised that when her principal wants to bring in new technology and change the way things are done in the library, Jane resists. In fact, she makes it nearly impossible to move forward with the project. The principal, once excited about the new equipment and all of the opportunities it will bring, is now putting it on the back burner. Every time it comes up, it becomes a difficult conversation with Jane, so much so that he avoids it as much as possible. It takes so much energy trying to convince Jane that this will actually enhance the library that it almost does not seem worth it. As a result, new technology from which teachers and students could really benefit sits in storage in its original boxes.

Jane is a resistor. She fears change because of what it might do to her comfort levels and control in her library. As a result, her negative energy around change makes it difficult for others to work with her and consequently results in delayed action for everyone involved. Because most people try to avoid conflict, dealing with Jane becomes a dreaded task that results in lack of action, conflict, and/or in slow progress. Resistance is our common defense system against fear, and change causes fear.

If you see yourself in this description of a resistor or you relate to "Jane," ask yourself the following questions:

1. What do I fear most about this change?
2. What thoughts am I having that are preventing me from moving forward?
3. What is the worst thing that can happen?
4. How am I serving or benefiting myself or others (including my students) by resisting change?
5. What benefits are in this change for my students? For me? How will my life be better?
6. How would it feel if I could move forward without these fears?
7. Who can support me and help me work through these challenges?

If you are working with a resistor and would like to help the resistor navigate change, the best way to deal with the fears and conflicting actions of a resistor is to help him see how the change will benefit them. This takes several steps, but saves considerable time in the long run. In Jane's case, the steps would include the following:

1. Have a conversation with Jane where you really listen to what is going on with her. What is really bothering her about this change? What is she afraid of? What things in the past may be contributing to her resistance?

2. Clarify her feelings and beliefs and try to determine what her biggest fears are around the change.

3. Validate her feelings and clear the defensiveness that she is putting up against you.

4. Help Jane overcome the obstacles preventing her from moving forward based on her expressed concerns. What things can you do to help her move forward? In this case, does she need training on the new equipment? Does she want to know how it will affect her schedules and procedures? Does she need to know how this will benefit her, her students, and her co-educators?

5. Follow through with your conversation with Jane. Whatever you said you would do to help her move forward, do it quickly. Keep your word and be consistent.

Resistors may be the last to come around, but from our experience, when they do, they buy in and support the change fully because of the process it took to accept the change. Even some of the "toughest cookies" will eventually come around. Honestly, it is usually one core thought or belief that holds resistors back. If you can identify and chip away at the core, your resistor can become your biggest ally. On the other hand, resistors are typically a small percentage of a school staff. So remember not to sacrifice fruitful work by focusing so much time and energy on one or two resistors.

The Reluctor

Reluctors will change when they feel ready or are pushed, but they change with much hesitation. Sometimes the reluctor changes once it becomes clear why the change is needed. Until the reluctor has the full buy-in, change is difficult. The reluctor's response to change is, "I'll do it if I have to!" Consider Pete, a middle school social studies teacher.

Pete has been pulling out his lesson plan book and following it to the letter every year for 10 years. He is considered a great teacher by his peers, and his students like him and do well in his classes. Because test scores for the school have been low, the school is adopting block schedule. This will allow teachers to have more time for hands-on work with their students, in hopes that differentiating the learning style will help students retain more knowledge. For Pete, this presents a problem. His lessons were created for a 50-minute period. He does not want to do extra work to fill the extra time and is complaining regularly to and with his peers. Because Pete is normally an easy-going guy and has many friends on the staff, others took on his attitude as well. The result is a lot of time spent complaining that could be used to enhance the lessons. The principal is feeling overwhelmed as more and more of the staff take Pete's stance. Telling the staff that the schedule change was going to take place and that they needed to adjust didn't seem to be working.

We have seen this example many times. If teachers think that something new is going to cause them a lot of time and discomfort, they are more likely to take on the role of a reluctor. Reluctors typically have easy-to-identify reasons for holding back when it comes to change. It may feel like it takes too much to overcome their reluctance, but taking the steps with one will likely spill over to other reluctors. When change is presented, it is common for many people to have shared concerns. Reluctors will listen to reason, when it is presented in a way that resonates with them. Taking time to listen to their concerns and help alleviate the primary concerns will make all the difference in your change movement.

Reluctors meet change with hesitation and some resistance. However, once the reluctor understands and accepts the reason for change, he or she can be the biggest promoter of the initiative.

Response Styles to Change

If you see yourself in this description of a reluctor or you relate to "Pete," ask yourself the following questions:

1. What thoughts am I having that are preventing me from moving forward?
2. How am I serving or benefiting myself or others with my reluctance and/or negativity?
3. Who can I talk to about my thoughts and get a clear understanding of the change and why it is happening?
4. What benefits are in this change for me? How will my life be better?
5. How does this help my students?
6. What support would help me get over this hurdle and where can I get it?

Reluctors may be dealing with events of the past, limiting beliefs, or fears that prevent them from seeing why change is necessary. Once they have discovered what is holding them back, they can pave the way to move forward. The best way to deal with the "reluctance" of a reluctor is to help him see why the change is necessary and the easiest way to make the change. This strategy is typically a bit easier than in a resistor because the reluctance is not embedded in fear. The steps to help Pete along might include the following:

1. Have a conversation with Pete to let him air his concerns. Listen to what he is saying and what the main conflict points are for him.
2. Determine what the main points are for Pete and think about what would help overcome them.
3. Show Pete how the change will benefit the students. This will help him at least feel like there is a good reason for it.
4. Show Pete (and others) easy and creative ways to adapt their lesson plans to help make the task feel manageable. If Pete doesn't feel like it is taking all of his time, he'll move forward more easily.
5. Ask Pete to share his experience with others. It is likely that once Pete is on board, his peers will be, too.
6. Use the solution that worked with Pete with everyone. For example, hold a special professional development session that gives teachers ways to adapt their lessons quickly and easily.

The Adaptor

Adaptors know that change is necessary, and they do it with ease. They may be the ones who make the change seem easy, or they may do it so easily they are not noticed at all. Sara is an example of an adaptor.

Sara's classroom bubbles with excitement and students who seem excited about learning. Sara has been teaching science for 12 years and is also involved with outside educational activities such as NASA's education programs for teachers. When something new is introduced to the staff, Sara quickly adapts it into her classroom and makes it work with her current instruction. Even though Sara is not quick to include things that are not a good fit for her classroom, she evaluates the pros and cons and often makes new programs work in ways that others haven't even considered. Because Sara is easy going and adapts to change easily, her innovative teaching strategies and ability to adapt are sometimes overlooked. In some cases, her peers feel intimidated by her ability to make everything "look so easy." This is especially true in times when others are showing reluctor tendencies. At these times, Sara does not "fit in" with the group.

If you relate to Sara when it comes to change, you are probably already thinking of ways to help others in the reluctor or resistor categories. Change may come easy to you, and you most likely enjoy making changes that help your students get more excited about learning. Use your positive attitude to help you go through the steps of this process and create the change that you are looking for right now.

Adaptors are great because they quickly take on new projects and opportunities. Sometimes, though, we can overlook adaptors. We may forget not only to appreciate them for the things that they do, but also to use their skills and attitudes to help with others. Some tactics that you can use with adaptors include the following:

1. Find out what they are doing. If it is working, and it usually is, you may be able to apply it to other teachers/classrooms.

2. Use adaptors to mentor or coach reluctors. If adaptors can help reluctors see the benefits of change, they will move forward more quickly. They can also teach others the strategies they are using in their classrooms.

3. Take time to recognize and appreciate adaptors. This need not be a major announcement, but take a moment to let them know that you see what they are doing and that you appreciate their efforts. A little gratitude goes a long way.

The Emotor

The emotor loves change and thrives on the adrenalin that comes with it. Emotors often seek change for the adventure or simply for the ups and downs of the process. Emotors tend to be on the excessive side of change—sometimes changing before they have completed their last change cycle. Consider Antonio.

Antonio is always excited. He loves to try new things and take on new projects. Antonio teaches English and poetry to high school seniors. His classroom is always an adventure, with projects and assignments that change from year to year. In his personal life, Antonio is always driving a different car and has moved several times in the past few years. He loves change and everything that comes with it. The down side to Antonio's change is that the projects go unfinished and that others get on board with an idea that he has, only to be left in the cold when they cannot follow his direction. Although Antonio's intentions are great and his students do well, he is considered "flighty" by some and even "hyperactive." When new change or tools are introduced in his classroom, he uses them sporadically. He is always willing to try new things and excited when new projects are proposed to him.

Emotors are like a diamond in the rough. They have great energy that should not be wasted, but many times it is hidden by their scattered appearance. Use this energy to your advantage! Who can't use a little extra help from a willing teacher or peer? That person can be your biggest asset if you are willing to tailor your approach to his needs.

If you related to "Antonio," never fear! You have a lot of excitement and energy, and you want to use it for the success of your students. One thing that may be valuable to you is finding an accountability partner or coach, depending on how much direction you seek. If you just want someone to make sure you are completing tasks and meeting your goals, a peer teacher as an accountability partner may be the solution for you. We often hear about

The emotor is always excited and ready to start the next project ...even before the last is finished.

accountability partners related to dieting or working out. Have you ever heard someone say she is more likely to work out if she has to meet someone at the gym? Knowing someone is holding you accountable makes you more willing to show up and then give it 100% while you are there. If you want more direction and someone who can work with you to create and follow through with your plan, a coach may be the avenue for you. Many schools now have coaching programs related to curriculum or technology support. Talk to your peers or your principal about how to find a coach who best fits your needs.

The emotor's energy is envied by some, but can become hard to manage or hard to follow for others. As a result, many times the emotor is not taken seriously because he "has a new idea every week." For managers of emotors, it may seem like it takes too much energy to work with the person. Emotors are excellent resources and motivators if you take the time to coach them. They typically make up the smallest percentage of a group, and there is usually one who comes to mind immediately. Managing tactics for the emotor include the following:

1. Help emotors get grounded. You can do this by helping them set goals for the project or task at hand. Emotors like to be successful and meet goals, but they rarely stop long enough to set them.

2. Put emotors on a strong team of leaders who will help focus the energy of the emotor, but not limit it.

3. Help the emotor see projects through to the end—for example, setting benchmarks and measuring throughout the year to keep up the momentum.

4. Maintain the excitement of the new programs or technology introduced to keep the emotor engaged versus using it sporadically.

5. Coach the emotor on how to be a better leader. Most emotors want to share their excitement with others. With a little coaching, they can be excellent leaders.

As a final thought to the four response styles, remember that a response style is just that, a style. Always consider the current situation versus categorizing yourself or your peers. We can change response styles based on the situation. For example, you might be a reluctor in a given situation because you have not determined why change is necessary, and an adaptor in another situation in which you are more comfortable. It is common to gravitate toward one response style, but it is important to not put our peers or ourselves in a permanent category.

Now that you understand response styles and what types of barriers contribute to them, you can move forward in your goal process armed with an understanding of what could get in your way and with tools to overcome those possible barriers. Sometimes, just this understanding deflates worry and anxiety related to a change process because we have had the chance to really think through what we want to accomplish and understand the cause of our anxiety. Take a moment now to remind yourself that you are strong and capable, and you will meet your goals. Think of your original vision of your perfect day and how you and your students benefit by the changes that you are making. Now let's move on to the next chapter and talk about how you can engage support as you achieve your goals.

Chapter Summary

A roadblock is less likely to bring you to a complete stop if you know that it is coming and you can plan another route. At this point in the change process, it is important to think about what could stop you from achieving your goals. What could get in the way of your end result? By thinking about those possible barriers to your success, you can plan ahead so that you have strategies to meet them.

• Reflections

1. *Think or refer back to the four response styles—"Resistor," "Reluctor," "Adaptor," "Emotor." With which style or styles do you relate?*

2. *What can you do to help yourself or others move forward, based on where you are in this process?*

3. *Now think about or refer back to the five common barriers to change. Look closely at each—Fear, Events of the Past, Attitudes and Limiting Beliefs, Resources and Time, and Self-Sabotage. Which of these gets in your way? What can you do to alleviate it so that you can be successful in achieving your goals? The more work you do in this area to really think about what could get in your way, the more likely you are to break through the resistance when it appears in your path to reaching your goals.*

chapter 8

Engage Support

People who are successful have one thing in common—they get the support they need when they need it. To be successful in your change initiative and meet your stated goals, you need support. In this chapter, we talk about personal accountability as you work

toward your goals and the external support that you need from others who can help you meet your goals. This includes support from your students, peers, administration, and parents. This may make you feel uncomfortable. If so, you are not alone. Time and time again, we hear that teachers aren't comfortable asking for support. You are accustomed to doing everything on your own and often do not want to step out of your comfort zone to ask for the resources or support you would like for your classroom. This chapter is intended to help you feel empowered to seek the support that you need.

Personal Accountability

You have made it through the first steps of the change process and now have goals that will help move you forward on your path. We hope you feel excited and ready to take action. Mixed with that excitement may be a little fear as to how you can really meet the goals you have set for yourself. This is the greatest challenge because it is so easy to second-guess yourself and lose track of what you hope to accomplish. There are specific ways that you can stay on track and be accountable to meet your goals.

The first way to stay on track is to create a personal accountability system—typically by finding a partner. No matter what your goals, it is important to have someone in addition to yourself who holds you accountable. An accountability partner should be someone who understands you, supports you, and will encourage you. You may find this person in the classroom next door, in the second floor math classroom, or even in your home. Whether this accountability partner is at school, at home or somewhere else entirely, you need to look for the person who will be most helpful in holding you accountable. It works well when you partner with the person who will check on you and hold you to deadlines that you agree upon. If you can return the favor for this person and work together toward your

A peer group is a great way to create accountability around similar goals. Members can provide support in many ways and hold each other accountable for actions.

goals, it will be a mutually beneficial relationship in which you both have a vested interest. If no one comes to mind immediately or if you just would rather not ask someone you know, think about going digital. Use the Internet to find a partner. You can do this by using education-based communities online. It may be a group that you join, or you may find ways to collaborate that you have yet to consider. If these sites are focusing on topics that relate to your goals, you will have extra resources and support to help you stay on track.

Another way to be accountable that works well in the school setting is the peer group approach. The math team or the second grade team may choose to provide peer group support for each other. The group can set regular times to update each other on their progress. The "peer pressure" for a positive outcome may give you the boost you need to stay on track with your goals. We were talking recently with a second grade teacher who transferred this year from teaching special education at the high school level. There is a huge difference between teaching second grade and teaching high school special education, even if you have elementary experience from the past. She mentioned that her entire second grade team stays after school to collaborate, share ideas, and coach each other. Because she and one of the other teachers are new this year this collaboration helps them form a cohesive approach to teaching and also provides extra support for the new teachers.

Although both of these suggestions provide strong support in helping you meet your goals, it is important that you do everything you can personally to stay focused. If you are not truly committed to reaching your goals, do not expect your accountability partner to do it for you. Keep your goals in front of you, posted where you will see them regularly as reminders to stay on track. Mark items on your calendar as milestones toward the steps you are taking to meet your goals. Start a journal to document your progress so you can review your progress and plan your next steps. Combining a personal system with an accountability partner or peer group will increase your odds for successfully meeting your goals.

Another trick that works well in the coaching world is creating a visual prop for your goals that you can discretely use as a reminder. For example, if your students keep you motivated, perhaps you use your class photo in a frame on your desk as a reminder of your goals.

Jill

"In a recent coaching session, my client said that she really wanted to learn to delegate work to her employees, so that she could focus on more 'fruitful' tasks. Together, we decided that she would put an apple on her desk to serve as a visual reminder of the way that she wanted to spend her time. To others around her, it was just an apple that she may have brought for lunch. To her, it was a visual cue to redirect to more fruitful work when she found herself working on something that could be delegated to employees."

External Support

Who can support me in this initiative? What do I need from them?

How do I approach them and ask for what I need?

We will help you answer those questions if the answers did not come to mind immediately. If they did, we will help you refine your answers and create a plan for follow-through to reach those individuals.

Whom Do I Need to Support Me in This Initiative? What Do I Need from Them?

Think about what you are trying to do—your vision (refer to the vision that you created in Chapter 5). What is the gap between your ultimate vision of success and where you are today? Who could be instrumental in the change that you want to see? Do you need verbal support within your school? Do you need resources? Do you need parental involvement? Asking yourself the right questions will help you decide who can be your most important allies in this process.

One of the biggest mistakes people make when they want to make changes in their lives is seeking advice from the people around them. Although it is comfortable and common to ask our friends and colleagues for advice, they are not always the best resources for the specific change we are trying to make. Although friends and colleagues may be ideal as accountability partners, it may be helpful to look outside of your normal circle when looking for mentorship or advice. Look for people, organizations, or schools that are already doing what you want to do and doing it well. What are they doing? How could they help you so that you can avoid starting from scratch? Partnering and/or learning from those who are already successfully doing what you want to do helps us expand our thinking, increase our creativity, and provide us with ideas we may not have come up with on our own. This requires extra steps, and sometimes those steps are outside of our comfort zones, but it pays off in the end. Einstein defined insanity as "doing the same thing over and over again, expecting a different result." Seeking advice from those already successful yields a *different* and *more positive* result every time.

The following outline can help you think through your specific situation. Take some time to think about the answers to these questions. You can use the end of the chapter summary and reflections section to write your answers in the space provided.

1. What is my ultimate vision for my classroom?
2. What goals have I set (short-term and long-term) for this process?

3. For each goal, list people or resources outside yourself that can help you achieve these goals. Tip: If no one comes to mind, do some research. Ask questions of your staff and peers; search online for experts who may be able to help. Reach out to your community to find out what kind of support exists that you have not considered.

4. For each of the people listed above, list specifically how they could help you.

5. Finally, make it even more specific by creating a list that has the names of the people and the organizations, what they can help with, and what specifically you need to ask of them. Do you need time, resources, money, public support, ideas, and/or mentoring? Even if it is not in your nature to ask for help, consider pushing yourself out of your comfort zone and asking for the support you need. People do like to be helpful, but many times they do not know how to help unless you ask.

● **Lydotta**

"I recently facilitated a session for several schools in Tennessee. Part of the session included principals sharing ideas about school improvement. All of the schools had similar issues; so by sharing stories about what was working, the principals gained strategies they could try in their own schools. Hearing about the success of their peers also gave them a sense of empowerment as it became clear that issues could be dealt with and changes made for improvement. The session was very energizing and helpful to everyone involved. Partnering and collaborating can be powerful."

How Do I Approach Them and Ask for What I Need?

Now that you know whom you want to approach and what you need to request, make a plan for following through. It is not always easy to ask for what we need, but those who do ask find much satisfaction and success. For each person or group that you listed, write down the best method to get in touch with them. Do you need to call and schedule a meeting? Will just a phone call do? If it is a group or organization, are there specific guidelines to follow? The answers to these questions depend on the people on your list and how well you know them. Only you know these answers.

When asking for what you need, be specific. People like to be resourceful to other people, and groups are accustomed to being approached for all different kinds of needs. If they are not able to help you, ask them to direct you to someone who can help.

Here are some examples of people and groups that everyone has in the district:

1. *Businesses*

What businesses do you have in your community that could help your school? How can you reach out to them and ask for what you need? Think beyond education partners into a community-wide education support effort. Businesses have the most to gain from education improvements because they are the ones relying on the labor pool for their bottom line. Some states or local communities even have a tax credit program for businesses who donate money and other resources to schools. Find out what your community has to offer. This may help you if you need specific resources for a project in your classroom. Often, a business needs only a request on school letterhead in exchange for providing you with resources you need.

You can take this one step further by really knowing the parents of your students. Where do they work and how can this help you? This could be part of an optional questionnaire at the beginning of the school year. Parents often want to help, but they don't know how to offer or may not even know what they have to offer. Finding out what they do, where they work, and even what their hobbies are can help you in the classroom. You may have a mother or father who likes photography and would be willing to come in and assist you with a lesson that makes use of digital cameras. You may have an electrical engineer who could come in and speak to the class about electrical currents. You may have a flower shop owner who would let you take a field trip to her shop to learn about entrepreneurship. There are so many ways to be creative if we just take a few extra steps that will provide us with resources and ideas.

Businesses in your community often have programs or funds in place to assist local schools but need direction and feedback as to how best to help.

2. *Community Groups*

What groups might you partner with to leverage support in the community? How can you create strategic partnerships that will be mutually beneficial? For example, we have opened Technology Opportunity Centers at schools across West Virginia. The purpose of these centers is to allow students and teachers to use computers during the day for instruction and community members to take computer courses in the evenings. Various groups in the communities have donated computers in exchange for special classes and services for their members. These groups are often looking for additional ways to get involved in the community. Approaching them with creative ideas that benefit students provides a win-win situation for everyone.

3. *Community Members*

Many people in your community could benefit your cause; they just need to be asked. Many small businesses and even retired individuals would love to help schools in some way. The key is asking for their support and being specific in your needs. For example, you could ask for volunteer time, bartering services, or even pro-bono services that can help move your cause forward. How do you find these people? Community groups, businesses, or even your students can provide you with names of people if they know what services or skills you could use in your classroom. Remember that this doesn't have to mean strangers coming into your classroom. Examples of support outside the classroom may include updating the playground, sprucing up the school grounds, donating old books or magazines for projects, or even sending in old photos or writings about something you are teaching in your classroom (events in history, natural disasters of the past, town histories, etc.).

4. *Parents*

Parents are your biggest constituents and in many cases, can make or break the overall environment of a school. Because of this, we have devoted a large section of this chapter to parent involvement.

Factoring Parents into the Change Process

We wanted to dedicate an entire section in this chapter to parents, because we know from our consulting experience that parents are central to the school. We have seen that parental involvement varies from school to school, but it almost always takes on a specific personality. Parental involvement makes a huge difference in all aspects of a school and from our experience, can make or break student motivation, teacher support, teacher motivation, and of course, discipline.

What Role Do Parents Play in the Change Process?

Why should you include parents as a component of the change process? Parents provide the foundation from which our students grow. Making them key players in

Parent involvement helps mold the culture of the school. Parents can be your biggest allies or in some cases your biggest challenge if they aren't involved in their children's education.

your change movement can facilitate easier communication, support students at home, and in some cases, even provide extra resources. How to involve your parents in the process depends largely on your specific community. The fact is no two schools are alike. Some districts have parents who are there for the students and the teachers and contribute regularly to the school. Other schools have parents who are barely involved with their children, much less the school that they attend. We realize that the latter makes involving parents in the change process difficult, and we hope to address some of those specific concerns.

Educating Parents about 21st Century Teaching and Learning

As discussed in Chapters 1 and 2, it is important to define what 21st century teaching and learning look like. After you are set with your definition and goals, you may need to educate your parents. How do you do this? We recommend creating a clear message that will be easy for parents to understand. Be sure that you emphasize what is different and why you feel the environment needs to be different. How you do it will depend on the frequency and modes of communication you use with your parents. Again, we realize this could be a challenge, for we have worked with schools where many of the parents are not responsive to school communication. If this is your situation, you may have to spend more of your time and resources on the "how" than on the "what" of educating them. You can use the following as a template for your parent communication plan. It is most effective if you can create your plan before the year starts, so you can start strong in the beginning when you have open houses, orientations, and other kickoff events. This plan can be modified to fit the entire school if you are working through this process as a school team.

Elements of an Effective Parent Communication Plan

1. Why do I need a communication plan? What results do I expect from creating and delivering the communication plan?

   For example, is your primary focus to educate about a new program? Gain support for a change? Increase parental involvement? Decrease student absenteeism? Your focus should represent your unique parent population and may even include all of these factors.

2. What is my message?

   The "what" includes the message that you want to give the parents. How will you communicate your vision and plans for your classroom? Although this is largely specific to you and your classroom, we believe the following components apply to almost all teachers with respect to the 21st century skills that we discuss. These are the concepts that should be conveyed to parents through the communication plan that you create:

   A. Why do we need to change the way we are doing things?

      - Illustrate the need for change in the school setting. The things that may have worked when they were in school are not working for today's students.

      - Provide examples about how things are different from when they went to school.

      - Consider your community's mindset and culture and tailor your message to that.

      - Use specific examples for the community, for example, new businesses, changing industries, students leaving after high school or college, and existing and future opportunities.

   B. What is a 21st century learning environment?

      - You can use the framework and video examples to describe what it looks like.

   C. What is your vision for your classroom (or school)?

   D. How can parents help? What do you ask of them?

   E. Call to action. What, *specifically*, do you need from them?

(continued)

Elements of an Effective Parent Communication Plan *continued*

3. How will I reach my parents?

What methods of communication will I use, and how often will I use them? How do I let my parents know the best times and ways to reach me? Do I connect by e-mail or phone message? Do I send information home with students? If you are creating this plan as a school team, we recommend a committee of teachers to help formulate a creative and strategic plan for your specific needs. The outcome of this step should be a clear action plan with steps to follow and deadlines to meet.

Modeling the 4Cs in Parent Communication

Parent communication and lack of parent involvement in education were two of the most reported challenges in our survey that teachers face daily. There are many reasons that parents may not be involved at the level teachers would like—apathy, lack of resources and transportation, low education level, lack of confidence, lack of time, role confusion, and poor communication. Some of these are superficial and easily overcome; others are more ingrained and difficult to change. Although low-income families are more commonly discussed with regard to low parent involvement, it was reported to be a problem in all areas of our "Greatest Challenge" survey. Some teachers even noted that they lived in wealthier suburban districts and still had low parent involvement. Regardless of the economic status of your students, we offer the following as strategies to help overcome this barrier.

As we have discussed, modeling the 4Cs as teachers is as important as teaching them to our students. Making real change in parent involvement takes time and focus, especially in schools that are starting with little or no parent support. Looking at parent involvement from the perspective of the 4Cs, think about how you can increase parent involvement at your school.

Critical thinking and *creativity* are the skills that we use to devise effective strategies to reach our parents and get them involved. Sending information home on a piece of paper and feeling frustrated when there is no response is an example of trying the same method repeatedly, expecting a different result. Take time to really reflect on your parent base. What is really going on? What do their lives look like? What might be holding them back from responding from their personal school experiences? Based on that, how can you best reach them and break through some of the barriers that are impeding their involvement in education?

Communication is at the heart of parent involvement. It may seem like common sense, but if you really want parents to be involved, the first step is to make them feel welcome and invited to participate. Parents are more responsive and more likely to be involved in their student's education if they feel like they are welcome to do so. For parents, feeling like they can easily contact their child's teacher or school can make a big difference in how much they participate. Being conscious of *how* you communicate with parents can go a long way in increasing their involvement. Making parents feel at ease and appreciated can translate to a better parent–teacher relationship and a better experience for your students.

What *method* of communication you use is also important in parent involvement. You are likely to reach more parents if you use multiple modes of communication. Parents use many types of communication, so using different methods to reach them increases your odds of getting your message delivered. Examples may include sending information home with students, updating your website, using e-mail, calling homes, calling cell phones, sending text messages, and using phone tree messaging systems. Some teachers are even using wikis and social networking to reach their students. You may feel like your parents do not have access to technology or cell phones. Ask them. We recently heard from a teacher at a middle school in a rural, low economic-status area. She sent home a survey about computer use in the homes and discovered that a higher percentage of families had access to the Internet than they assumed based on the economic conditions of the area. In our experience, parents and students are becoming quite creative and savvy when it comes to obtaining computers and cell phones. The key point is to use multiple strategies and be consistent so that you can determine what works best with your particular group of parents.

How can you send the message to parents that you want them to actively participate in what happens in your classroom? How can you ask for support? In some areas, where involvement is lowest, extra measures for ***collaboration*** may need to be taken. These may include home visits and parent workshops to really reach the parents.

A parent or guardian's involvement in a child's education and day-to-day activities results in multiple benefits for not only the student, but also the parents and educators.

Factoring Parents into the Change Process

Getting Parents Involved

These are parent involvement strategies that we collected from teachers. Use these examples as they are or use them to inspire you to create your own!

The Apple Tree—Similar to the concept of the Angel Tree, teachers put needs for their classrooms on "apples" that are hung on a tree cutout in a central place in the school. Parents can take an apple off the tree and pick up something for the teachers. This is a great idea for the holidays too, so teachers receive gifts that they need and want for their classrooms.

The Parent Wiki—Create a school wiki that facilitates parental communication and allows for a form of interactivity. This is not unlike the website that you have, except that parents can add and edit too, creating a community versus an online brochure. Another component to this could be a place where parents share special skills and knowledge that could help the students for career research and extra learning opportunities and help teachers have a resource for classroom presentations, resources, and so on.

Pizza and Planning—Schedule one night per quarter to sit down with interested parents on a variety of breakout topics focusing on a list that parents have identified. By suggesting topics, parents will become part of the solution. It is easy to identify issues, but harder to find the answers. If the parents are there and engaged, they can participate in solutions and add a new perspective.

Sharing through Sports—Many times parents who may not always attend school functions can be found at the community centers during different sport seasons. By setting up casual information centers at these locations, you can share information with parents who may not feel comfortable in a school setting because of their personal experiences as students or other reasons.

Rise and Shine Parents Assembly—Parents are invited to a school "Rise and Shine" assembly every Friday morning. The school showcases a different class each week, and every student in the class gets a turn at the microphone. Most parents love sharing their children's moments in the spotlight! Every Friday may be too much, but maybe you could try once a month.

We recently conducted a series of parental involvement workshops in which we shared ideas to help parents relate to their middle school child. Together, parents and their children attended the workshop, which focused on helping middle school children stay on track with school. We shared ideas about organizational skills, time management, clear expectations, limits and boundaries, and staying connected to each other and the school. We also discussed the importance of helping your children set goals and serving as their accountability partner(s). We found the format of the workshop, as well as the suggestions and activities, to be well accepted by those who participated. Most had not participated in a workshop like this together. If you have not held parent involvement workshops, we suggest coordinating them with sporting events or the distribution of student schedules to encourage parents to attend. Be creative as you plan and think about the best ways to reach the greatest number of your parents. You may even consider incentives such as small stipends or prizes to increase the number of parents who may not otherwise attend.

Dealing with a Really Difficult Parent Base

What do you do when you have a really difficult parent base? Often this is seen in poorer economic areas where communication is the significant challenge. Parents do not have reliable modes of communication (phone, Internet) in some cases, and many are not interested or are not in a place in their own lives when they feel like they can be involved in their children's school life. Our suggestion would be to start small. Find a base of parents who are interested in being involved, but may need some "coaching" to get over their own fears. We know that when parents are not educated or had negative experiences in school, they may worry that they do not have what it takes to play a role in the school. Again, creating a team of teachers to specifically address this could have a valuable payoff. It may take time and many one-on-one conversations to get these parents on board. You could also offer classes or workshops off school grounds to try to get the parents to start the process of being educated in what you are trying to do. We know this can be a difficult and frustrating situation, but with time, we believe it can improve.

So now that you have come to this point, think about your overall plan for engaging support for your goals and the changes you are making. The following is a summary of the questions you can answer to create your plan of action:

1. Whom do I need to support me in this initiative? Parents? Other teachers? Administrators? Local businesses? Community members? Other?

2. What do I need from them?

3. How will I approach them and ask for what I need?

4. What is the current parent involvement level with my parents?

5. What level would I like for that to reach?

6. Why is parent communication important?

7. What do I want my parents to know about my classroom and my goals?

8. What is my communication plan for parents?

9. Who will commit to helping me with the parent component?

10. How will we do it and on what time line?

Once you answer these questions, you can begin putting your plan into place. Asking for help can be difficult, but it can make all the difference for you in what you are trying to achieve in your classroom and school.

Chapter Summary

People who are successful have one thing in common: they get the support they need when they need it. To be successful in your change initiative and meet your stated goals, you need support. Accountability helps people stay on target and not put their goals on the back burner. By constructing vehicles for accountability, you create clear expectations and a way that your team can support each other. Accountability can come in the form of coaching, mentoring, training, pairing teachers, and forming teams. How will you create accountability for your goals?

● Reflections

1. What kind of personal accountability will you create for this process? Determine how you will create this before you finish this book. No matter what your goals are, it is important to have someone in addition to yourself who holds you accountable. An accountability partner should be someone who understands you, supports you, and will encourage you.

2. Answer the questions below and within the chapter about external support and create the resulting list with action items.

   • What is my ultimate vision for my classroom?

   • What goals have I set (short-term and long-term) for this process?

   • For each goal, list people or resources outside yourself that can help you achieve these goals. Tip: If no one comes to mind, do some research. Ask questions of your staff and peers; research the Internet for experts who may be able to help. Reach out to your community to find out what kind of support exists that you have not considered.

- For each of the people listed above, list specifically how that person could help you.

- Finally, make it even more specific by creating a list that has the person or organization's name, what each one can help with, and what specifically you need to ask of them. Do you need time, resources, money, public support, ideas, and/or mentoring? This list could go on and on, and we know from experience that you do not like to ask for help. It could make the difference in your time spent and the results that you wish to achieve. Even if it is not in your nature, consider pushing yourself out of your comfort level and asking for the support you need. People like to be helpful, but many times they do not know how to help unless you ask.

3. Think about your parent base. How involved are they in the education process? How could they be more supportive? Involved? What do you want from those relationships in your classroom?

   List some activities you can implement immediately to get parents more involved or supportive of learning and what is happening in your classroom.

chapter 9

Make It Real in Your Classrooms—Ideas for Student Engagement

Throughout this book, we have focused on change, goal setting, and culture. We have also asked you to focus on what these mean to you, your classroom, and your students. It is now time to put your ideas into action. No matter what goals you set, chances are that each of them has a connection to your classroom. This chapter provides examples of

student engagement, implementation of 21st century skills, and ways to step out of your comfort zone to make learning real for your students and for you. Although these ideas may not match your subject area exactly, we hope that they will generate thoughts on how you can make the learning experience real in your classroom and fulfill your goals. We also provide steps for modifying and recreating curriculum units for your content and grade levels.

We see you as the expert because you know your students best and you know what works for their learning. We provide ideas in this chapter to inspire you and help you get started making changes to your teaching strategies. You can begin this process by asking yourself the following questions:

- "What would it look like if I changed the way I teach?"
- "What ideas have I had that I have never followed through with in my classroom?"
- "How would my students benefit if I take my teaching to the next level?"

We get trapped in our old ways of thinking and day-to-day habits and routines. To break these habits, take a moment to stop at any point during your day of teaching and ask yourself, *"How could I do this differently?"* Our hope is that this chapter takes your thoughts and goals from throughout this book and helps you step out of your comfort zone and turn those thoughts into actions. We encourage you to not only use these examples, but also modify them according to your expertise, resources, and subject matter. We will talk about steps you can take to modify your curriculum later in this chapter.

Creating Relevance for Students

The most important part of any goal related to classroom instruction is what happens when you close your classroom door. To be sure that new tools and strategies are implemented in a meaningful way, you must "make it real" or create relevance for your students and yourself. When teachers create relevance, students are engaged in the learning process. Today's students want to be active and engaged learners and participants in the classroom. They want to know how the content is related to the "real world." How will they use this knowledge, and when will they use the knowledge after they graduate? As they move through their daily routines, they enjoy working in teams, solving problems, using technology, and researching information. Another benefit to student engagement is a better learning and teaching environment with fewer discipline problems and classroom management issues. Students who are actively working and learning are less likely to be disruptive because of boredom or lack of interest.

Determining how to create this 21st century learning environment can be challenging in the already-busy days of teachers. Teachers know what they need to teach and how many demands there are for the time they have with their students. Often, it is difficult to determine new ways to engage students while meeting all of the other expectations. We clearly understand that challenge. On a positive note, our digital world provides us with limitless resources, activities, and lessons for the classroom. Although it may take some time to determine which activities tie to your standards and meet your classroom needs, it is often helpful to look at what other teachers and students are doing to implement 21st century skills and engage students in their classrooms.

According to REL Appalachia, *Schools of the Future: Driven by Technology*, technology will play a large role in designing and building productive learning environments of the future. In its discussion of schools of the future, the document emphasizes the need for open, accessible spaces with flexible design to connect learning. These schools may have classroom settings that are used part of the day for face-to-face instruction and part for virtual learning. More and more online education and connections will allow students to learn from anywhere at any time. Many interesting articles and research are referenced in this document as ideas about what schools of the future hold for our students. As teachers, we can use this information to help us prepare our students for the future and to inspire us as we teach in our current classrooms. To read the entire brief, visit www.cna.org.

A Look at 21st Century Teaching and Learning in Practice

Engaging classrooms in every country are preparing students with the skills to live and work in a fast paced, ever-changing global world. From elementary schools to high schools, teachers are creating new ideas and changing their teaching strategies to engage students. The following examples range across K–12 and include brief ideas, detailed lesson ideas, stories from individual teachers, and research briefs that show the success of 21st century instruction.

21st Century Scientists

The iPad can be used in almost every aspect of a science classroom and easily aligned with the 21st century framework. A typical high school science class can seamlessly use the iPad as the textbook, calculator, reference sheet, and Internet browser integrating media literacy with science curriculum. The iPad can also be used as a data collector during experiments and then used to type a lab report that is submitted to the teacher via e-mail, demonstrating collaboration, critical thinking, and self-direction. The iPad can also be used for various online assessments. This is all achieved with one piece of equipment with no classroom time lost in transitioning from one activity to another. When choosing technology, we can easily buy several gadgets, each with a single function, but the iPad is a single piece of technology with numerous functions. It is the "Swiss Army Knife" of teaching and easily aligns with 21st century skills and tools.

Communicating and Collaborating to Explore Energy Careers

Social networks and other online and related technology tools play a central role in the lives of K–12 students. Social networks provide constant communication and continuous sharing for individuals of all ages as we are connected on a larger scale than ever before. Many teachers have asked, "Why not use this communication method as a way to engage students in the learning process?" The example below does exactly that in a protected environment that includes all the features of a standard social network.

My Next Horizon, a social network, was created so students could explore topics and careers in science, technology, engineering, and mathematics. On the site, students interact with each other, while simultaneously exploring new topics that will prepare them for the 21st century workforce. Students sign on, personalize their profile page, network with mentors, and ask them for advice about science-, technology-, engineering-, and mathematics-related careers. A teacher choosing an implementation such as this can use this opportunity to discuss and review Internet safety and digital citizenship before allowing a student access to the site. An agreement between the student and teacher focused on creating and maintaining a positive online community emphasizes the importance of acceptable use and citizenship. The following story clearly illustrates how the social network is being used in the classroom.

A group of middle school students participated in a mentor event with oil and natural gas industry experts to ask questions and learn more about careers in this field. The event was a great way to connect students with professionals in an environment where they felt comfortable. From the convenience of their offices, the mentors could speak candidly and informally with students, sharing information and answering questions on a variety of STEM topics. This event allowed the mentors to reach students whom they would never have had a chance to meet personally. Opportunities like this can be life changing for students and shape their future in ways they may not have considered.

To try this in your classroom, visit one of the many social networking, wiki, or blog sites to design and build your own social network for your students. Protect the site and allow access to only the participants whom you approve.

Engaging Students in Civic Literacy

A focus on civic literacy is a key part of 21st century skills. Determining ways to link students to the community can be a challenge, but one that can be rewarding and educational for everyone involved. The following example shows how one Advanced Placement English teacher linked her students to a community organization in need using collaboration, creativity, and communication skills.

Ms. Kuskey, an Advanced Placement English teacher, asked her students to design public relations materials for a local foundation that focuses on preservation of a wool farm. The goal of the project was to promote the 21st century skill, civic literacy, creating a link between the AP students and their community. The foundation needed assistance in public relations and was excited to work with local students to achieve the foundation's goal. This was a unique opportunity for students to interact with community members. The students chose at least one of the project options to complete the assignment: radio and television public service announcements (PSAs), a two-fold color brochure, PowerPoint, or a movie-maker film.

The students were placed in teams and required to have team meetings and work closely to clearly define, design, and implement their project. Each group also worked closely with the foundation board and staff. The students toured the foundation house and collected information needed to complete the assignment. Ms. Kuskey followed the model from Ted McCain's book, *Teaching for Tomorrow: Teaching Content and Problem-Solving Skills*.

Coursework that requires students to collaborate and solve real-world problems addresses both core content and 21st century skills.

A Look at 21st Century Teaching and Learning in Practice

Through this process, students were required to create digital products that would be used by the foundation. This project was completed in three lessons: Defining the Project, Designing the Project, and Implementing the Project. Students were responsible for evaluating their own work. The teacher used wikis and blogs throughout the project to track progress. This project was a win-win situation for the students and the foundation because everyone gained from the process and the end product.

Creating, Collaborating, and Communicating with a Flip Camera

Scenario: You attend a workshop and walk away with a flip camera for your classroom. Question: How do I use this 21st century tool to engage my math students in a meaningful way?

The list below describes a variety of different uses that are simple and engaging:

- Students record each other explaining solutions to problems.
- Students record the steps to solving a word problem including explanations and/or demonstrations based on the grade level.
- Students interview famous mathematicians (students can research and role-play).
- Students interview community members who use math in their jobs.
- Students search for math in nature and in everyday items and places such as a parent's workplace.
- Students create a "Math in the Real World" video (e.g., HotChalk® video, "Off-Road Algebra") or a math rap video.

Rubik's® Cube—Perhaps a Surprising 21st Century Classroom Application

The Rubik's® Cube brings back memories for many of us, and it also brings back engaging activities and a creative way to approach critical thinking, problem solving, and the ability to work as part of a team. A geometry class begins by exploring hexominoe nets. Students first define and label the polyhedron (Rubik's® Cube): face, edge, and vertex. Students are then placed in small cooperative groups and measure the dimensions of a cereal box. As a class, each group collaborates to cut the box open so it is one flat piece of cardboard. Groups label the faces with the appropriate dimensions and compare and discuss the nets. (A hexominoe net is a two-dimensional representation of a three-dimensional shape. If folded correctly, it will form a cube.) The students then calculate the total area of the box and make a conjecture about a formula for finding the area of the cereal box.

After becoming familiar with hexominoe nets, the groups then examine the Rubik's® Cube and are presented with the following question—"How many small cubes make up a 3×3×3 Rubik's® Cube?" Each group has time to take the cube apart, put it back together, and then create its own Rubik's® Cube from nets. Students will use the graph paper to design 26 hexominoe nets and fold each into a cube. Each group places all cubes together to form one large cube and color each side of the cube to match that of the Rubik's® Cube and displays for all to see.

Exploring Music in Video Games—A Music Lesson Using Creativity and Innovation

The following example focuses on a successful music lesson that integrates 21st century tools, creativity, critical thinking, and problem solving. Students use the Internet to research two different programs: *The Video Game Musician* and *The Jingle Writer*. The students then write —definitions for linear music, interactive music, jingle writer, jingle shop, copyright, public domain, and musicologist in their notes. A class discussion is held on how music works in a video game, and students share singing several of their favorite jingles. The discussion continues on what makes these tunes memorable. The teacher then assigns the following activities:

- Create a video game based on a familiar story. Create a storyboard with four to six scenes depicting what will happen in your game. You will need to compose music that demonstrates what is happening in your game, or you can choose songs that show linear and interactive music from music that you already have. You will need to research the music and find out which company owns the rights to that song. You will need to write a letter to that company, asking for its permission to use that song and explain how and why you are using it.

- You are going to advertise a product that you use every day or that you think no one would be using. Write a short skit using the jingle that you create. If you use background music, you must research the company owning the rights to that song and write a letter requesting permission to use it. If your jingle is a parody, you do not have to write a letter, but you must write out your parody.

This example provides a music teacher with a very different 21st century approach to music class. Numerous variations on this lesson could engage students in other subject areas.

Scale Drawings—A Hands-On Approach to the 4Cs

Students in this math classroom were asked to research special effects in film and television and hold group discussions on how scale proportions are used by means of

The creative use of film and television took this math lesson out of the classroom and onto the big screen, with the 4Cs as the feature presentation.

critical thinking and collaboration skills. The teacher then shares, *Honey, I Shrunk the Kids*, *Indian in the Cupboard*, or *The Borrowers* to discuss how scale is used to make the actors look small.

The teacher then uses a map to show an example of a scale drawing. The students locate and measure the scale on the map. Next, the class moves into a project creating scale drawings of real objects that allow them to answer the following question: "How can you make a prop for a movie so it looks like an actor your size has been shrunk to the size of your action figure?" The project is designed to take two to three class periods including group presentations.

Students are assigned to heterogeneous groups and given a variety of action figures (4–5 inches high). Students work through a variety of activities measuring the action figures. Groups are provided instruction through a handout or a wiki directing them to measure the action figure and assign one person in the group as the "actor." The group then compares the actor and the action figure to determine the proportion ratio. This allows the group to have the necessary measurements to create the prop. Students then randomly select an object from a bag and apply the ratio to complete a scale drawing. Students choose various methods of constructing their props considering size and appearance in their choices. Final group presentations are given to the class, including the ratio calculations.

Cast Your Opinion—Using the Cell Phone as a Tool for Engagement

In any subject area where students are placed in groups and asked to create a product, you can easily use the online tool polleverywhere.com. In a recent professional development session where groups of teachers designed a product using the 4Cs, the participants used polleverywhere.com to cast their vote for the best product. The site is easy to use and requires only a cell phone. This is an engaging way to integrate technology, critical thinking, and communication into a lesson.

The Corporate Classroom—Real-World Collaboration and Critical Thinking

At a middle and high school, Rick Kinder, a dedicated math teacher, is integrating 21st century skills in a unique way that he created. His initiative, "The Corporate Classroom," not only has helped him change his mathematics instruction, but also has allowed him to keep up with the ways that students process information. His approach uses T-MESH (Technology Incorporated with Math, English, Science, and History) and a corporate business–type culture where students are integrating technology and 21st century skills in a cross-curricular fashion. The classroom becomes a business structure and students use math skills in core content areas. The class functions as a business and has its own web page. The web page contains everything a student needs for the class and the business.

Throughout the class, Mr. Kinder uses a variety of instructional strategies unlike the ones he used in the beginning of his teaching career. Instead of working through the textbook, he begins with what the students know and builds on that foundation. Throughout the semester, students will see the same topics over and over, but in different forms. The problems get harder as the semester progresses. Every topic is related to an experience they can understand. This is true for basic math as well as Algebra II. He includes topics focused on a car purchase that includes insurance quotes and the use of the quadratic formula, property taxes, and gross and net pay. Making the students think and build on what they already learned in a business environment makes this class engaging for students.

Hybrid Algebra I—A Research Brief Example

Learning algebra becomes more of a challenge the later we take it in high school. Finding creative ways to teach the content also becomes more challenging. A panel of math teachers and district respresentatives stepping up to that challenge described their approach, Hybrid Algebra I, at a recent conference. This approach highlights critical thinking and collaboration.

Hybrid Algebra I includes sustained professional development for teachers as well as instructional materials and recommended classroom practices. The program uses a blended approach (hybrid) to instruction for both teachers and students. This 21st century example takes place in a traditional, face-to-face classroom with access to Algebra I instructional software. The learning environment included a mobile lab, personal laptops, and a lab setting outside of the actual classroom.

Hybrid Algebra I combines multiple modes of teaching, learning, and professional support to ensure that all students and teachers have the tools and skills that they need to succeed in the program.

The intervention uses online resources in face-to-face technology-enhanced classrooms to facilitate the use of Algebra I standards-based instructional practices and to improve student learning in grade 9 Algebra I classrooms. Each student spends at least 40% of class time using online courseware (such as 2 days a week in a computer lab for a course that meets 5 days a week or 40% of each period when classroom computers are available). When students use the computers, the teacher acts as a coach, assisting individual students or providing mini-lessons to larger groups of students as needed. The use of blended instructional practices is expanding rapidly in Kentucky, where this group originated, and nationally.

Teachers in this program have access in their classrooms to online instructional resources for direct instruction. Participating teachers engage in sustained professional development focusing on effective Algebra I pedagogy and the use of technology to improve instructional practices and student learning. Professional development takes place in blended classrooms as well as online. It begins in the summer and continues through the school year, with monthly, online-facilitated discussions among participating teachers and two follow-up classroom visits by math instructional specialists (content example from REL-A Technical Brief www.cna.org).

Prepositional Phrases in Action

This example is a creative way to compare adjective and adverb phrases. This lesson was created by a middle school teacher teaching grades 5 through 8. The goal of the lesson was to use still action photos and then write captions with prepositional phrases. Students started the lesson by going around the school and taking action shots. Students were using multiple modes of communication and technology skills as they took and uploaded the photos.

The students then wrote captions for each photo using adjective/adverb prepositional phrases. They next identified prepositional phrases and labeled those applying grammatical and mechanical properties in writing. After completing these activities, the students color-coded the phrases and presented them to the class.

The Edible Schoolyard

We would be remiss if we did not include an example from Edutopia™ (www.edutopia.org) in our list. Rich with outstanding resources for teachers, the site is one that we use in training sessions and workshops for teachers and students. One of many favorites, *The Edible Schoolyard*, was used years ago as part of a school year kick-off presentation. *The Edible Schoolyard* is a video of an elementary classroom that actually grows vegetables and then harvests the crop to make a pie using math calculations, measurement, and collaborative teamwork. The video is very well done and extremely inspiring. As we reviewed the video for our presentation, Lydotta's daughter, a high school student at the time, stated, "I would be a teacher if I thought teaching could be like that video." That statement really resonated with us as we thought about our work with teachers and future teachers. Think about how you can do something engaging with your students that might inspire your students to want to become teachers.

Reading/Language Arts Menu Encourages Self-Direction

In the third grade classroom of Ms. Pastorius, the students are required to read. *The Sun, the Wind, and the Rain*. The related assignments are given to the students in the form of a menu. Each group of students must complete two main dishes, one side dish, and one dessert by the end of the week. The main dishes include the following options:

- Make a chart comparing and contrasting the real mountain and the sand mountain in the story, *The Sun, the Wind, and the Rain.*
- Pretend you are at the beach and write a letter to a friend telling how you built a sandcastle.
- Pick 5 spelling words and write a sentence for each using context clues.

Side dishes include these choices:

- Make a "Wanted" poster for a character from the story including a drawing of and information about her or him.
- Draw a picture of the ideal sandcastle and then write a paragraph about what makes it so special.
- Write a journal entry with the title, "A Day at the Beach."

Desserts include these activities:

- Write a song or poem about the story.
- Pretend you are a TV news anchor. With the rest of the class as your audience, tell them the details of the storm.

Presenting this common assignment in an uncommon fashion has the student involved in choosing his or her path for learning (self-direction).

Gaming in Education to Promote Critical Thinking

Video games are sometimes regarded as a "waste of time," requiring little intellectual capacity; however, research reveals that educational gaming not only offers meaningful and challenging learning environments, but also quite effectively aids in the development of cognitive skills and engaging experiential learning opportunities. "Programs offering exploratory environments—databases, simulations, hypermedia-based programs—enable **students** to take active control over their **learning**" (Rosas et al., 2003). There are various uses and benefits of standards-based gaming for the development of successful and progressive 21st century learners.

Several games are available for a variety of game systems and grade levels. Examples of classroom applications include games for the Wii™ to motivate students to not only collaborate and communicate effectively with each other, but also become more physically active. Wii™ Sports can be used to develop or enhance math skills or to meet physical education standards. Many elementary teachers are using Wii™ Sports in the classroom to compare scores using ratios, estimation and predictions, probabilities, and more. Elementary and middle school students love these applications because they actively engage them in learning and calculating math concepts.

Middle and high schools use games such as *The Trauma Series* or *Cooking Mama* in content areas such as chemistry and consumer sciences. Students steadily develop skills as the game progresses, thus increasing student comprehension and ability as they move forward in the game. Other games, like those found online, can be used with the interactive whiteboards to create a virtual and interactive environment for student learning in the classroom.

Gaming helps develop critical thinking and problem solving skills, as well as communication and collaboration skills. Gaming is a way to engage students who feel bored in classrooms lacking visual stimulation and to help students needing more practice in critical thinking and problem solving. The use of gaming in the classroom has proved that learning can indeed be fun, while promoting and enhancing essential skill development. *Don't Bother Me Mom—I'm Learning* by Marc Prensky is an interesting reference addressing this topic.

iPod Touch in the Kindergarten Classroom

When we started writing this book, Ashton was 3 years old. As we finish this project, he is 5 and well into kindergarten. One day after school, he was talking about what he had done during the day. He was excited because he used an iPod Touch to play games that taught letters and math–a perfect example for this chapter. Ashton's teacher, Mrs. Akers, is known for her engaging methods of instruction and use of energy and movement in keeping her students motivated to learn. Ashton's classroom has been a great example of 21st century teaching and learning to us in the final stages of writing this book.

"Making It Real" in Nontraditional Schools and Other Education Environments

The integration and focus on 21st century skills is not limited to the normal school day or specific curriculum. An example of 21st century skills implementation in a nontraditional setting is happening in the Boys & Girls Clubs of Western Pennsylvania. In many after-school programs operated by the Boys & Girls Clubs, a curriculum entitled *After*

Movement and creative activities keep students engaged and excited about learning.

School Excellence is being used. State and national standards in K–8 math and K–3 reading were blended with 21ˢᵗ century skills, large- and small-group activities, computer software, and assessments to create an engaging and focused after-school curriculum. Students use critical thinking, problem solving, life skills, financial skills, and global awareness as they work through an engaging curriculum that assists them in doing additional work on content standards.

This design has proved to be successful as students have the opportunity to play games, utilize manipulatives, use technology, and focus on skills that need extra emphasis. Employing a 21ˢᵗ century focus, students enjoy participating and learning. The same is true in similar summer programs that engage students in the learning process.

Get Your Creativity Flowing

Now that we have shared some detailed examples, we also want to share other ideas to help you think about ways to integrate the 21ˢᵗ century skills, themes, literacies, and outcomes into your teaching. This is about transforming your teaching and meeting the goals that you have worked on throughout this book. The following list gives you some great ideas to do just that:

- Have students *tweet* as they collect data in a science project.
- Try *Glogster* for online student development of multimedia posters.
- Use *Garage Band* to enhance vocabulary word studies or reports and presentations.
- Try *Math Snacks* for extra help with math topics.
- Create or have your students create an infographic (graphic or picture to quickly display information or data) to share information.
- Use digital storytelling to transform your science classroom.
- Try a ready-to-use or do-it-yourself applet to make your content more engaging.
- Use Web 2.0 tools to create digital citizenship projects for journalism classes.
- Use *EDU 2.0* or *Symbaloo EDU*.
- Check out *Edublogs* or *Kidblog*.
- Use *Collaborize Classroom*™ to allow class discussions on topics after class.
- Have students produce the media that are used throughout your school.
- Look at open source platforms that can help you enhance your classroom at no added cost.
- Check out Voice Thread for the collection of group conversations, images, documents, and video.

Tie It All Together: Steps for Modifying and Re-Creating Curriculum Units

If you are ready to transform your lessons, these simple steps will help you get started. Choose one or two of your favorite lessons and follow the steps below. By beginning with something you have really enjoyed teaching, you will find the effort of transforming the unit more enjoyable.

1. Select a favorite lesson that you teach.

2. Review the standards that are part of this lesson.

3. Determine which of the 4Cs, skills, and literacies could easily fit into your lesson.

4. Research and create ways to integrate the skills you have selected.

5. Modify your lesson to integrate the applicable 21st century skills and literacies.

6. Test with students, determine effectiveness, and make adjustments for future implementation.

If you want to create new units and corresponding lessons, use these steps:

1. Determine a new idea that fits in your standards that could also tie into the 4Cs or any of the 21st century skills such as global awareness, or one of the literacies or life skills.

2. Determine the content standards that you would like to teach with the selected 21st century skills.

Earlier in this book, we mentioned our 1998 Technology Innovation Challenge Grant from the U.S. Department of Education. Through this project, we developed *www.thesolutionsite.com*, a free resource with thousands of units and lessons for teachers. This site has been updated continuously and includes many units that focus on 21st century skills. We have added resources from classroom teachers through private foundation funding, the National Science Foundation, the U.S. Department of Transportation, and a variety of other sources.

One of the National Science Foundation projects was a partnership with West Virginia University College of Engineering that created *TIME Kits* for education. *TIME Kits*, Tools for Integrating Math and Engineering, are standards-based curriculum units that integrate a real-world engineering problem into the math and science curriculum. A middle school teacher of gifted students recently shared this thought with us on the use of the *TIME Kits* in her classroom. "Last year I used several *TIME Kits* with my students, and they would always come in at the beginning of class and say, 'Do we have to do math today or are we going to get to do a *TIME Kit*?' It made me laugh because EVERY Kit we did was full of math concepts— teaching, applying, and assessing multiple math

content standards and objectives—but they didn't look at them like that. They looked at them as fun engineering projects. I've always thought some of the best learning moments were those that came in disguise. And sure enough, at the end of each *TIME Kit*, almost all of my students had improved scores on their post-tests. *TIME Kits* prove time and again, they are fun *and* effective."

3. Create an outline of your idea integrating the 21st century framework with the content standards.

4. Create your unit(s) and corresponding lesson.

5. Test with students, determine effectiveness, and make adjustments for future implementation.

Continue Learning through Professional Development

Although examples and resources are valuable to "Making It Real in the Classroom," the key component for success is ongoing professional development. The typical school day is very demanding and pulls the classroom teacher in many directions. The opportunity to work with other teachers in professional development settings is imperative to sustaining classroom change. This development can be completed in a variety of ways. Some teachers prefer face-to-face instruction; others prefer the online option, which allows them to work when they want and at their own pace. Another approach includes a blend of online and face-to-face training. One thing that continues to be clear is that a one-day overview does not provide what teachers really need. Teachers want to network, share ideas and resources, and be engaged in professional development. Professional learning communities are becoming more and more helpful in many districts across the country because of their focus on bringing teachers together and allowing them to think, share, and act upon their discussions. These communities provide a network of colleagues the opportunity to work on issues, participate in training programs together, and support each

Professional learning communities are becoming more and more popular among educators because they promote sharing and collaborating as key components to professional development.

other. Having a team or community to share and move forward with can be very effective.

ISTE—International Society for Technology Education—is an outstanding organization dedicated to supporting the use of information technology to aid in learning and in teaching K–12 students and teachers. At *istelearning.com*, teachers become ISTE Learners continuing to grow and contribute to education technology. Visit ISTE U, the ISTE Café, or the Learning Lab to network, share, and learn with other educators from around the world. You will find ISTE a great place to connect and learn.

No matter which delivery method is used, the focus should be on practical, hands-on, engaging sessions that help teachers learn skills that benefit students. We have found that teachers like to be engaged and taught in the same way as the 21st century student. When learning opportunities are fun and engaging and allow participants to share ideas and discuss the future, they are meaningful and worthwhile. Education and learning are constantly changing. If teachers continue to stay abreast of the most effective methods and tools, our education system will be strong and our students will ultimately benefit.

Although we strongly suggest formal professional development, we also realize that funding for professional development may not be available. We know that this makes it difficult for busy teachers to grow and learn. Many teachers with whom we have spoken say they believe in and enjoy professional development, but lack of time and/or funding prevents this from happening in their school or district. Many learning and sharing opportunities can be done online. For example, ISTE and INTEL are two great resources with excellent online professional development opportunities. The Partnership for 21st Century Skills Route 21 and content maps include many examples of how to use 21st century skills in your classroom. Visit www.p21.org to find details. Route 21 specifically includes resources around the 4Cs ranging from rubrics to classroom examples. Many districts, schools, and individuals have shared research and real-world applications that make it easier for you to get started. If you decide to focus on more collaboration in your classroom, you can find rubrics on Route 21 to help you. Sign up and check out the resources that apply to you.

Further, the members of P21 have unlimited resources, some of which are free and can provide you with additional ideas. The following is the list of P21 members: American Association of School Librarians, Education Networks of America, Knowledge Works Foundation, Adobe, Pearson, Apple, Blackboard, Cable in the Classroom, CENGAGE Learning, CISCO Systems, Crayola, Dell, ETS, EF Education, Global Scholar, Houghton Mifflin Harcourt, Hewlett Packard, Junior Achievement, Learning Point, LEGO, McGraw-Hill Education, Measured Progress, MHZ Networks, Microsoft, National Academy Foundation, National Education Association, net Trekker, Oracle Education Foundation, Project Management Institute Educational Foundation, Verizon, and The Walt Disney Company. Many of these members offer resources and activities for education at little or no cost to teachers. To learn more, visit their respective websites.

Take Action—One Step at a Time

The challenge of "Making It Real in the Classroom" can seem a bit overwhelming, depending on where you are in your classroom instructional methods and strategies. Be encouraged and inspired by the examples and ideas you are reading in this book. Focus on the importance of doing something different in the classroom for the students you serve and for yourself. Students who are engaged and excited about learning will make your job easier and more rewarding. It is important to remember that everyone who has achieved goals has moved forward one step at a time. Find a mentor, look for resources, try one new activity, start off with a creative project, and begin with something that you feel comfortable facilitating. Whatever you decide, try not to get overwhelmed. Most often the students understand if things do not go right the first time, and they welcome the new idea that you are attempting.

It is also important to work together with others in your school for advice, ideas, and support. Find peers who are doing the things you want to do—talk with them, seek their advice, use their ideas of what works in the classroom. Help fellow teachers as they branch out and try new things. The more you do as a team, the more enjoyable the entire process is for everyone and the better the classroom environment is for your students. Team-teach with colleagues and be there to support each other. Decide the best way for you to communicate, and use traditional methods or technology to connect and stay connected with each other. By trying just one of these ideas, you will be on your way to building an engaging and rewarding 21st century classroom.

Celebrate Your Milestones and Successes

It is essential that you look regularly at how far you have come and celebrate. Remember that it is not just the destination, but the journey that makes you successful in evolving to a 21st century learning environment. The more fun the journey, the more you and your team will want to continue building and growing. Think of ways to celebrate along the way. Create milestones where you can stop and enjoy the progress that you have made.

Take this time for yourself. Create a reward system. This looks different for everyone. Some like to reward themselves with time spent on something enjoyable, while others use a physical token—something they purchase to show they have achieved a goal. No matter what you choose, remember that celebrating is as important as the journey itself. In our *Who Took My Chalk?*™ schools, we see reasons to celebrate and so do the teachers. It is encouraging to watch teams work through and move beyond issues to implement stronger and more engaging learning environments for their students. When the stress of underlying issues or uncertainty is gone, teachers feel better and enjoy their teaching even more. So celebrate your accomplishments and move forward!

● Jill

Many times my coaching clients reach milestones and achieve results in their life, only to look forward to the next. It always takes them by surprise when I ask them how they are going to celebrate what they have achieved.

Congratulations! You now have a step-by-step plan and many tools with which to get started on your journey. You are well on your way to creating the change that you wish to see in your classroom or in your school. We wish you success as you begin this journey, and we hope that you will share your knowledge with others on the path to creating change in education. Most of all, we thank you for all that you do as a teacher for our students every day. You change lives and make a difference. For that we are grateful and hope that this book has been helpful to you.

Chapter Summary

The most important part of any goal for classroom instruction relates in one way or another to change and what happens when you close the classroom door. To be sure that new tools and strategies are implemented in a meaningful way, you must "make it real" for students and yourself. When teachers "make it real," students are engaged in the learning process. Today's students want to be active and engaged learners and participants. As they move throughout their daily routine, they enjoy the excitement of working in teams, solving problems, using technology, and researching information. When students are active, they are more in tune with the information they are learning.

● Reflections

1. Reflect on the following questions from the beginning of the chapter:

   • What would it look like if I changed the way I teach?

- What ideas have I had that I have not followed through with in my classroom?

- How would my students benefit if I take my teaching to the next level?

2. Look at the examples of student engagement in this chapter. Choose two examples that you could apply in your classroom either as they are or with modifications. Make the necessary modifications and preparations to implement the idea in your classroom. Determine how the idea/activity aligns with your content and curriculum and create a time line for implementation.

3. Choose three units that you have been teaching regularly. Modify the units based on your goals set in this process or on 21st century concepts and ideas from this book or related research. Make the necessary modifications and preparations to implement the idea in your classroom. Determine how the idea/activity aligns with your content and curriculum and create a time line for implementation.

Book Study Guide

The purpose of this chapter is to provide you with a workbook that can be used in a book study for your school team should you choose to work through the *Who Took My Chalk?*™ model together. Each section provides you with a short chapter summary and the reflections and actions associated with that chapter. By the end of this book, you should have an outline of steps to take given the specific challenges you face and the goals you want to achieve. Depending on how you structure your time, you can complete one (or more if time allows) section(s) each time you meet as a group and take action steps (homework) between meeting times. During your face-to-face time, you may choose to report on your actions and discuss the reflection questions as a group. This will ensure that you are working together as a team, sharing ideas, and also taking action and creating intentional change between meeting times. As we have said throughout this process, each school and each classroom is different, so choose a structure that works for your unique environment. The important thing is that you commit to the process and follow through with that commitment to your successful outcomes.

CHAPTER 1 *The World Is Changing*

We know that the world looks different through the lens of our students—whether they are in pre-K, elementary, middle school, or high school. We looked at ways they communicate with friends, plan activities, share information, and run their lives, and we see that those ways are very different from the world that we as their parents and teachers experienced. Even as adults, we live in a different world now, compared to when we were in school. The pressure is growing for teachers to prepare students for jobs and careers that do not even exist today, as depicted by the careers that Gary Marx projected in his book *Sixteen Trends. . . Their Profound Impact on our Future*. We know and have evidence of these changes, and now we must act on them by changing the way that we teach. We must build upon the things we are doing well; we need to reconstruct or stop using the strategies that are not working and take our skills and expertise to next level—creating 21st century learning environments in which our students thrive.

Thinking about both the generational research in Chapter 1 and your own experience since you started teaching, reflect on the following—first personally, then share as a group and discuss.

● Reflections

1. *Why did I choose teaching as a career?*

2. *How have education and the way I teach changed since I started teaching?*

3. *How have my students changed since I started teaching?*

4. *What passion, expertise, and skills do I have that will help create change in my classroom and in my school?*

CHAPTER 2 *21ˢᵗ Century Skills and a Model for Change*

The shift to integrating and teaching 21ˢᵗ century skills begins with setting the stage for change, creating a culture of acceptance for change, and setting intentions for the change to take place. Once that foundation is laid, 21ˢᵗ century skills can be integrated. The *Partnership for 21ˢᵗ Century Skills* has clearly defined and set the stage for 21ˢᵗ century skills in the classroom through the 4Cs—communication, creativity, communication, and critical thinking and problem solving.

Who Took My Chalk?™ is a model that sets the stage for change. The eight steps of the model include the following:

1. Recognize the need or desire to change.
2. Assess your school culture and your personal attitude.
3. Set and achieve 21ˢᵗ century goals.
4. Communicate clearly.
5. Predict possible roadblocks.
6. Engage support.
7. Make it real in your classroom.
8. Create and finalize your plan for success.

● Reflections

After answering the questions defined in the 21ˢᵗ Century Classroom Assessment Tool, respond to the following, first individually, then together as a school team.

Is Your Classroom a 21st Century Classroom?

Please answer each question by circling the "Yes" (Y), "No" (N), or "Sometimes" (S), depending on the frequency of that activity in your classroom. The questions you answer "No" or "Sometimes" are good places to start as you begin thinking about goals

Collaboration

1. Do you teach and encourage collaboration and teamwork in your students?   Y   N   S

2. Do you have units or lessons that require students to work in teams to complete?   Y   N   S

3. Do your students collaborate with you and each other to solve problems and create products or solutions?   Y   N   S

4. Do your students assume shared responsibility for collaborative work?   Y   N   S

5. Do your students work together as a team, while learning to value the individual contributions of the members?   Y   N   S

Communication

1. Do your students use a variety of communication skills in your classroom (oral, written, nonverbal)?   Y   N   S

2. Do your students participate in lessons or activities in which listening is a key component?   Y   N   S

3. Do your students openly communicate with you and one another in your classroom?   Y   N   S

4. Do your students share ideas, dialogue, and debate in your classroom?   Y   N   S

5. Is your classroom one in which students feel safe to express ideas and can communicate openly?   Y   N   S

Creativity (and Innovation)

1. Do your students have the opportunity to be open to new and creative ideas from their peers?   Y   N   S

2. Are your students rewarded by you for creativity and "thinking outside the box"?   Y   N   S

3. Do your students engage in creative, activity-based learning in your classroom?   Y   N   S

4. Do your students have a process to create and evaluate new ideas in your classroom?   Y   N   S

5. Do you teach your students to learn from "mistakes," "failures," or strategies that do not seem to work?   Y   N   S

Critical Thinking and Problem Solving

1. Are your students empowered to know how, when, and where to seek knowledge and find answers to questions?   Y   N   S

2. Do your students take an active part in decisions in their learning?   Y   N   S

3. Do your students have the opportunity to analyze and evaluate different points of view?   Y   N   S

4. Do your students engage in activities where they interpret information and draw conclusions?   Y   N   S

5. Are your students engaged in lessons and activities in which they work to solve problems and devise creative solutions?   Y   N   S

Use of Technology as a 21st Century Tool

1. Do your students have the opportunity to use various technologies as tools for learning in your classroom?   Y   N   S

2. Do your students have the opportunity to use many types of media throughout their learning processes?   Y   N   S

3. Do you integrate technology into your curriculum in a way that encourages the use of technology as a tool, rather than a stand-alone skill?   Y   N   S

4. Do your students use computers to help them seek information and gain knowledge?   Y   N   S

5. Do you integrate your students' experience with technology (computers, cell phones, social networks) into your teaching strategies?   Y   N   S

BOOK STUDY GUIDE

As a group, respond to and discuss the following questions:

1. *What did you learn from the assessment? How were you surprised?*

2. *In which of the five areas did we have the most number of "YES" answers? "NO" answers?*

3. *In which areas are we strong as a school? How can we build upon what we are doing well?*

4. *How did the group results differ from individual results? (Individuals share similarities or differences between their individual responses and the overall school responses.)*

5. *On which areas should we focus the most effort as we begin the shift to modeling and teaching 21st century skills in our classrooms?*

6. *Reflecting on the eight steps of the* Who Took My Chalk?™ *model, respond to the following:*

7. *What were your first impressions of the model? What do you hope to obtain from the model as you progress through the steps in this book?*

CHAPTER 3 *Recognize the Need or Desire to Change*

If we think about the habits we develop as we go through our everyday routines, we realize that it is necessary to focus consciously on doing things differently to create change and growth in our life. Many times our predisposed notions of how things are limit us from dreaming about how they could be.

Why are you reading this book? Did you want to make a change or did something change in your environment that brought you to this point? Think about the common school scenarios that call for change. Are any of those affecting your school right now? Discuss those scenarios or situations as a group. Make a list of all of the things that are creating the need for change in your school.

Our School Scenarios that Call for Change

1.

2.

3.

4.

5.

● **Reflections**

1. *Assess your attitude by answering the following questions. How would we categorize the overall attitude of the teachers, staff, and administrators at our school? What types of conversations do we engage in as colleagues? How do those attitudes and related moods affect our students? How can we tell?*

2. *Make a list of the ways that your attitudes are manifested in your students.*

3. *Looking back to the "thought-feeling-action" cycle, what habits have you developed in your thoughts as a staff that are contributing to your feelings and resulting actions? Think about your staff meetings.*

    a. *What are the key messages or issues that are discussed?*

    b. *What feelings result from these discussions and themes?*

    c. *What action is taken as a result?*

4. *What kinds of change do we **intend** to create in our classrooms?*

5. *What kinds of fears surface for you when we think about changing our teaching styles and our classrooms?*

6. *How can having a positive attitude help us overcome those fears? What other things might help push us out of our comfort zones and help us overcome any fears we have about implementing 21st century skills in our curriculum?*

CHAPTER 4 *Assess Your School Culture and Environment*

Twenty-first-century teaching and learning calls for a new school culture that supports students, teachers, and administrators in the learning process. Our definition of school culture focuses on six characteristics for schools—student engagement, collaboration, goal setting, action planning, assessing attitude, and engaging openness. Most schools do not dedicate enough time to focus on these characteristics or give teachers the chance to address issues to improve the work environment. Many teachers feel that their voices are never heard and that schoolwide communication around culture is rarely discussed because of the many demands and challenges that exist on a daily basis. The following reflections and activities will help you take this time to reflect on the culture of your school and the culture that you create in your classroom.

● Reflections

1. *What does your school culture feel like? Is it positive, allowing students to have positive experiences, opportunities, and achievement? Is it negative, causing a block in creative, academic, and extracurricular opportunities? What areas could be improved?*

● Activities

1. Complete the "Chalkboard of Challenges & Impacts" as a school team (only the part described at the end of Chapter 4).

2. List the challenges you determined through this activity.

   1.

   2.

   3.

   4.

   5.

6.

7.

8.

9.

10.

CHAPTER 5 *Set ... and Achieve Goals*

As we think about teaching in the 21ˢᵗ century, it is easy to realize that as we strive to adjust our instruction to meet the needs of today's students, we need to set and achieve goals to guide us through these evolving times. A recap of the SMART Goal process follows:

	SMART Goals	
S	**Specific**	What do you want to achieve?
M	**Measurable**	How will you know when you reach it?
A	**Attainable**	Is it possible and worth striving for?
R	**Realistic**	What resources do you need? How will you do it?
T	**Time-Oriented**	By when will you achieve it?

Use the reflections and activities in this chapter to determine your *Energy Wasters* and *Energy Savers* and create the goals that have resulted from your assessment. Follow the steps to achieve your goals and create the results you want in your classroom.

● Reflections

1. *Assess your Chalkboard of Challenges & Impacts*

Based on the discussion in Chapter 5, list your *Energy Wasters* below, along with the estimated amount of time you spend on each per week.

Energy Wasters

Energy Wasters	Amount of Time Spent Per Week
1.	
2.	
3.	
4.	
5.	

Now based on the discussion of *Energy Savers* list those below.

Energy Savers

Energy Savers
1.
2.
3.
4.
5.

After you have determined your *Energy Savers*, prioritize them in the order you would like to address them. It is from this list that you will develop your goals.

Energy Savers—In Order of Highest Priority

Energy Savers—In Order of Highest Priority
1.
2.
3.
4.
5.

2. Visualize the End Result—Complete the visualization activity from Chapter 5 as a group by answering the questions below.

- In what kind of school do we teach? How are the environment and school culture?

- What do our classrooms or learning environments look like?

- What kind of tools and resources are available to us to teach the way we want to teach?

- What roles do we play as the teachers?

- How do our students interact with us? Each other?

- How engaged are the students? What is the mood and feel of the environment?

- How involved are the parents at our school and in what ways? How do they support us in our teaching?

- What types of instruction do we use to teach our students?

- What ultimate outcomes do we desire for our students?

- How do we feel when we leave our school at the end of the day?

3. Reflecting on your *Energy Savers* list and the visualization that you just completed, use the table on the next page to list three to five goals you would like to accomplish as a school team (see the example below). Under each goal, create the steps it will take to reach the destination. These steps will provide you with a clear chronological path to reach your goal. Start with the goal and work the steps down from largest to smallest. Using the steps, create a time line to help you map out the steps of the goal over the school year (or longer for the long-term goals).

Goal-Setting Example

Goal #			
Integrate technology and the 4Cs into one curriculum unit per semester.			
Action Needed	**By When?**	**How will I do It?**	✓
Determine units to modify	*End of next week*	*-look at units to determine which would lend best to the use of technology*	☐

Goal-Setting Template

GOAL 1:			
Action Needed	**By When?**	**How will I do It?**	**✓**
			☐
			☐
			☐

GOAL 2:			
Action Needed	**By When?**	**How will I do It?**	**✓**
			☐
			☐
			☐

GOAL 3:			
Action Needed	**By When?**	**How will I do It?**	**✓**
			☐
			☐
			☐

GOAL 4:			
Action Needed	**By When?**	**How will I do It?**	**✓**
			☐
			☐
			☐

GOAL 5:			
Action Needed	**By When?**	**How will I do It?**	**✓**
			☐
			☐
			☐

4. *Achieve Your Goals!*

Choose at least one of the success strategies under Goal Achieving and commit to it. Follow the steps described to take action today! Use Goal-Setting Template to track progress and make adjustments as needed.

CHAPTER 6 *Communicate Clearly*

Most educators chose their profession because they feel or felt that they could make a difference in the lives of children, and ultimately, in the future of our society. Communication is central to everything. In schools, communication (or lack thereof) can create a path to success (good communication) or be the cause for conflict and demise (bad or no communication). Using coaching skills with students, peers, and administrators can help create better communication in our schools. Teaching students about how to use communication tools effectively is also a key component to embracing *communication* as one of the 4Cs in our schools.

● Activity

1. Refer to the coaching skills in Chapter 6. As a group, choose partners for this activity. Choose one skill and apply it in your conversations and interactions for the next day. Partners can practice the skills with each other and also share experiences of how it worked with others.

Reflections (to Share with Partner)

1. *What did you notice about infusing the skill into your daily interactions?*

2. *What experiences resulted from using the skill that may not have occurred had you not used the skill?*

As a group, discuss the following questions:

3. *How can we integrate 21ˢᵗ century communication tools into our curriculum?*

4. *What type of protocol or etiquette do we think is important for our students to understand with respect to 21ˢᵗ century communication tools?*

5. *What types of communication tools can we integrate into our classrooms for our students?*

CHAPTER 7 *Predict Possible Roadblocks*

A roadblock is less likely to bring you to a complete stop if you know that it is coming and you can plan another route. At this point in the change process, it is important to think about what could stop you from achieving your goals. What could get in the way of your end result? By thinking about what those possible barriers to your success might be, you can plan ahead so that you have strategies to meet them.

● Reflections

1. *Think or refer back to the four response styles—"Resistor," "Reluctor," "Adaptor," "Emotor." With which style or styles do you relate?*

2. *What can you do to help yourself or others move forward, based on where you are in this process?*

3. *Now think about or refer back to the common barriers to change. Looking closely at each—Fear, Events of the Past, Attitudes and Limiting Beliefs, Resources and Time, and Self-Sabotage—which of these gets in our way as a school team? What can we do to alleviate it so that we can be successful in achieving our goals? The more work you do in this area to really think about what could get in your way, the more likely you are to break through the resistance when it appears in your path to reaching your goals.*

CHAPTER 8 *Engage Support*

People who are successful have one thing in common—they get the support they need when they need it. To be successful in your change initiative and meet your stated goals, you need support. Accountability helps people stay on target and not put their goals on the back burner. By constructing vehicles for accountability, you create clear expectations and a way that your team can support each other. Accountability can come in the form of coaching, mentoring, training, pairing teachers, and forming teams. How will you create accountability for your goals?

● Activities

1. What kind of personal accountability will you create for each other as a team in this process? Determine how you will create this before you finish this book. No matter what your goals are, it is important to have someone in addition to yourself who holds you accountable. An accountability partner should be someone who understands you, supports you, and will encourage you. As a group, determine how you will serve as accountability partners for one another. One suggestion is to break into small groups to focus on specific tasks or goals and within that group, break into pairs for personal accountability. This creates both one-on-one and group accountability.

2. Answer the questions below and within the chapter about external support and create the resulting list with action items.

a. What is our ultimate vision for our classrooms?

b. What goals have we set (short-term and long-term) for this process?

c. For each goal, list people or outside resources who can help us achieve these goals. Tip: If no one comes to mind, do some research. Ask questions of our staff and peers; research the Internet for experts who may be able to help. Reach out to our community to find out what kind of support exists that we have not considered.

d. For each of the people listed above, list specifically how that person could help our team.

e. Finally, make it even more specific by creating a list that has the person or organization's name, what each one can help with, and what specifically we need to ask of them. Do we need time, resources, money, public support, ideas, and/or mentoring? This list could go on and on, and we know from experience that we do not like to ask for help. It could make the difference in our time spent and the results that we wish to achieve. Even if it is not in our nature, we must consider pushing out of our comfort level and asking for the support we need. People do like to be helpful, but many times they do not know how to help unless we ask.

● Reflections

1. *Think about your parent base. How involved are they in the education process? How could they be more supportive? Involved? What do you want from those relationships in your classrooms?*

● **Activity**

1. List some activities you can implement immediately to get parents more involved or supportive of learning and what is happening in your classrooms.

CHAPTER 9 *Make It Real in Your Classroom—Ideas for Student Engagement*

The most important part of any goal related to classroom instruction ties in one way or another to change and what happens when you close the classroom door. To be sure that new tools and strategies are implemented in a meaningful way, you must "make it real" for students and yourself. When teachers "make it real," students are engaged in the learning process.

Today's students want to be active and engaged learners and participants. As they move throughout their daily routine, they enjoy the excitement of working in teams, solving problems, using technology, and researching information. When students are active, they are more in tune with the information they are learning.

● **Reflections**

Reflect on the following questions:

1. *What would it look like if we modified or enhanced our teaching methodology?*

2. *What ideas do we have that we have not followed through with in our school?*

3. *How would our students benefit if we take our teaching to the next level?*

● Activity

Look at the examples of student engagement in Chapter 9. Brainstorm as a group to create a school theme, by which you will apply the following steps in every classroom, with each grade level making the appropriate modifications.

1. Determine a new idea that fits in your standards that could also tie into the 4Cs or any of the 21st century skills such as global awareness, one of the literacies or life skills.

2. Determine the content standards that you would like to teach with the selected 21st skills.

3. Create an outline of your idea integrating the 21st century framework with the content standards.

4. Create your unit(s) and corresponding lesson.

5. Test with students, determine effectiveness, and make adjustments for future implementation.

Create a time line that the group can follow. You can also use creative ideas from the list at the end of Chapter 9 about getting your creativity flowing. For example, have students create signage and media to post throughout the school to support the theme. Get parents involved in the process as much as possible too. This is a great way to kick off your 21st century skills initiative and educate parents about the process at the same time.

Celebrate Your Milestones and Successes

It is essential that you look regularly at how far you have come and celebrate as a team. Remember that is it not just the destination, but the journey that makes you successful in evolving to a 21st century learning environment. The more fun the journey, the more you and your team will want to create! Think of ways to celebrate along the way. Create milestones where you can stop and enjoy the progress that you have made. You are well on your way to creating the change that you wish to see in your classrooms or in your school. We wish you success as you begin this journey and hope that you will share your knowledge with others on the path to creating change in education.

references

Center for Naval Analysis. (2010, August 19). *Schools of the future: Driven by technology*. Retrieved from http://www.cna.org/centers/education/rel/tech-assistance/reference-desk/2010-08-19

Cluckyful. (2010, February 19). *Shift happens 2010* [video file]. Video posted to http://www.youtube.com/watch?v=TZjRJeWfVtY

Edutopia. (2004, March 11). *The edible schoolyard yields seed-to-table learning* [video file]. Video posted to http://www.youtube.com/watch?v=TZjRJeWfVtY

Entrepreneur. (n.d.). *Corporate culture*. Retrieved from http://www.entrepreneur.com/encyclopedia/term/82104.html

Fredrickson, B. L. (2004). The broaden-and-build theory of positive emotions. *The Royal Society*, 359(1449). Retrieved from http://rstb.royalsocietypublishing.org/content/359/1449/1367.full.pdf+html?sid=41935742-a6d8-4625-81ad-32accf5715d1

Gladwell, M. (2000). *The tipping point: How little things can make a big difference*. Boston: Little, Brown and Company.

Haudan, J. (2008). *The art of engagement: Bridging the gap between people and possibilities*. New York: McGraw-Hill.

High, J., & Andrews, P. G. (2009). Engaging students and ensuring success. *Middle School Journal*, 41(2), 58–63.

Hill, N. (2008). *Think and grow rich!* Clemson, SC: The Mindpower Press.

Jayson, S. (2004, October 12). Power of a super attitude. *USA Today*. Retrieved from http://www.usatoday.com/news/health/2004-10-12-mind-body_x.htm

Marx, G. (2006). *Sixteen trends and their profound impact on our future*. Alexandria, VA: Educational Research Service.

Maxwell, J. C. (1999). *The 21 indispensable qualities of a leader*. Nashville, TN: Thomas Nelson, Inc.

McCaine, T. (2005). *Teaching for tomorrow: Teaching content and problem-solving skills*. Thousand Oaks, CA: Corwin Press.

Morisano, D., Hirsh, J., Peterson, J., Pihl, R., & Shore, B. (2010). Setting, elaborating, and reflecting on personal goals improves academic performance. *Journal of Applied Psychology*, 95(2). Retrieved from http://www.selfauthoring.com/JAPcomplete.pdf

Ostroff, C. (1992). The relationship between satisfaction, attitudes, and performance: An organizational level analysis. *Journal of Applied Psychology*, 77(6), 963–974.

Partnership for 21st Century Skills. (2004). *Our history*. Retrieved from http://www.p21.org/index.php?option=com_content&task=view&id=507&Itemid=191

Partnership for 21st Century Skills. (2004). *Our mission*. Retrieved from http://www.p21.org/index.php?option=com_content&task=view&id=188&Itemid=110

Peters, L. W. (1988). *The sun, the wind and the rain*. New York, NY: Henry Holt and Company.

Phillips, G. (1993). *What is school culture?* Retrieved from http://www.schoolculture.net/whatisit.html

Prensky, M. (2006). *Don't bother me mom—I'm learning*. St. Paul, MN: Paragon House.

Proctor, B. (2001). *The goal achiever*. Scottsdale, AZ: Lifesuccess Productions.

Radar, L. (2005). *Goal setting for students and teachers: Six steps to success*. Clearing House, 78(3), 123–126.

Raines, C. (2009). *Generations at work*. Retrieved from http://www.generationsatwork.com/index.php

Rosas, R., Nussbaum, M., Cumsille, P., Marianov, V., Correa, M., Flores, P.,& Salinas, M. (2003). Beyond Nintendo: Design and assessment of educational video games for first and second grade students. *Computers & Education,* 40, 71–94.

Tapscott, D. (1998). *Growing up digital: The rise of the net generation.* New York: McGraw-Hill.

US Department of Labor, Bureau of Labor Statistics. (2010). *Number of jobs held, labor market activity, and earnings growth among the youngest baby boomer* (USDL-10-1243). Washington, DC: US Department of Labor. Retrieved from http://www.bls.gov/news.release/pdf/nlsoy.pdf

Whitworth, L., Kimsey-House, H., & Sandahl, P. (1998). *Co-active coaching: New skills for coaching people toward success in work and life.* Palo Alto, CA: Davies-Black Publishing.

appendices

The following resources were developed by The Partnership for 21st Century Skills by Lydotta Taylor, Susan Saltrick, and Ken Kay. Multiple resources are provided for each of the 4Cs.

- *Appendix A: Professional Development Resources: The 4Cs*
- *Appendix B: Professional Development Resources: Critical Thinking and Problem Solving*
- *Appendix C: Professional Development Resources: Creativity and Innovation*
- *Appendix D: Professional Development Resources: Communication*
- *Appendix E: Professional Development Resources: Collaboration*

Professional Development Resources
The 4Cs

All of the following resources are aimed at helping teachers promote the 4Cs—critical thinking, creativity and innovation, communication, and collaboration skills—in their students.

ONLINE PROFESSIONAL DEVELOPMENT PROGRAMS & RESOURCES
Intel Education. Intel offers free, easily integrated tools and teaching resources to support collaborative student-centered learning—including online thinking tools for students and teaching resources such as lesson plans, assessment strategies, and technology-enriched project ideas for all K–12 subjects. Developed by educators, these free tools and resources support 21st century learning in the classroom. http://www.intel.com/education/teachers/
Intel also offers three free online PD courses: *Collaboration for the Digital Classroom, Assessment in 21st Century Classrooms,* and *Project-based Approaches.* http://www.intel.com/education/elements/index.htm

Verizon offers a free 1-hour Webinar for educators that introduces 21st century skills, explains why 21st century skills are so important for today's students, and shows how to access thousands of free Verizon Thinkfinity resources that support 21st century learning. http://community.thinkfinity.org/community/professionaldevelopment?view=iframe&frame =http://tims.thinkfinity.org/CourseSessions/coursespecificregistration.aspx?CourseID=96

PBS Teachers. This website, aimed at K–12 teachers, offers a rich array of multimedia resources, lesson plans, and activity packs for classroom use, as well as blogs, webinars, and online courses for professional development. http://www.pbs.org/teachers

PROFESSIONAL DEVELOPMENT PROGRAMS
Antioch University–New England: *Critical Skills Program.* The AUNE website provides information on their 3- and 5-day personal development (PD) programs, as well as books on assessing and coaching the 4Cs. Free classroom tools that support student learning and teacher facilitation of these skills are also available. http://www.antiochne.edu/acsr/criticalskills/

Project Zero: *WIDE World:* Based on research from Harvard Graduate School of Education, these research-based, job-embedded, online professional development programs foster the creation of professional communities of teachers and school leaders and equip them with the knowledge and skills they need to cultivate the critical 21st century learning needs of their students. http://learnweb.harvard.edu/wide/en/index.html

BOOKS

William M. Ferriter & Adam Garry: *Teaching the iGeneration: 5 Easy Ways to Introduce Essential Skills With Web 2.0 Tools.* This SolutionTree publication helps teachers promote their students' information fluency, persuasion, communication, collaboration, and problem solving skills. Each chapter presents a digital solution that can be used to enhance traditional skill-based instructional practices, as well as of handouts and supporting materials. http://www.solution-tree.com/Public/Media.aspx?ShowDetail=true&ProductID=BKF393

Ted McCain: *Teaching for Tomorrow: Teaching Content and Problem-Solving Skills.* The author provides a step-by-step process for challenging students to engage more deeply in their learning and become more critical and creative problem solvers.

Heidi Hayes Jacobs, ed. *Curriculum 21: Essential Education for a Changing World.* Edited by the renowned curriculum expert, with contributions from 10 other expert educators, this book offers guidance in transforming schools into 21st century learning organizations.

Jay McTighe & Grant Wiggins: *Understanding by Design: Professional Development Workbook.* This professional development guidebook extends the ideas of UBD and offers a comprehensive array of template, tools, and work samples to guide teachers and leader in their application of *Understanding by Design*, the highly regarded approach to curriculum design that focuses on deepening students' understanding and building their capacity in the 4Cs.

Bernie Trilling & Charles Fadel: *21st Century Skills Learning for Life in our Times.* This book provides an excellent overview of 21st century skills and what they mean to everyone involved in education as we move forward. The volume comes with a DVD of classroom examples of teaching and learning that focus on 21st century skills development.

James Bellanca & Ron Brandt: *21st century skills Rethinking How Students Learn.* This SolutionTree publication features a collection of articles related to 21st century skills from the most prominent experts in 21st century teaching and learning.

Guofang Wan & Dianne M. Gut: *Bringing Schools into the 21st Century.* This book explores issues related to transforming and modernizing our educational system including the impact of societal shifts on education.

Professional Development Resources
Critical Thinking And Problem Solving

Reason Effectively
- Use various types of reasoning (inductive, deductive, etc.) as appropriate to the situation

Use Systems Thinking
- Analyze how parts of a whole interact with each other to produce overall outcomes in complex systems

Make Judgments and Decisions
- Effectively analyze and evaluate evidence, arguments, claims, and beliefs
- Analyze and evaluate major alternative points of view
- Synthesize and make connections between information and arguments
- Interpret information and draw conclusions based on the best analysis
- Reflect critically on learning experiences and processes

Solve Problems
- Solve different kinds of nonfamiliar problems in both conventional and innovative ways
- Identify and ask significant questions that clarify various points of view and lead to better solutions

PROFESSIONAL DEVELOPMENT: The following resources help teachers understand how to promote the creativity and innovation skills of their students.

VIDEO
ITC Publications: *The TeacherPD Video Series.* This Australian company has produced 20 excellent short videos of teachers demonstrating proven classroom techniques and activities that promote students' critical thinking skills. ITC also publishes teacher diaries and posters that provide critical thinking exercises and strategies. http://www.itcpublications.com.au/

ASCD: *Learning to Think … Thinking to Learn.* PD activities designed for large-group workshops, small study groups, and individual study that help teachers promote three major types of thinking skills: information processing skills, critical thinking skills, and complex thinking strategies, with lessons from elementary, middle, and high school classrooms. http://shop.ascd.org/productdisplay.cfm?productid=607087

ONLINE COURSE
Critical Think
This course is designed to give teachers an opportunity to develop unique teaching methods and strategies. Both the reading and writing assignments are varied and extensive. Learning to think, learning to extract ideas and support your ideas in the public forum is not always easy, but well worth doing. If you can read, think, and express yourself clearly, you have mastered the skills of a lifelong learner. For more information, visit www.theedventuregroup.org

BOOKS & E-BOOKS
Microsoft, in association with ISTE: *Developing Critical Thinking through Web Research Skills*. This e-book features lesson plans that include prerequisites, rationale, essential concepts, and descriptions of related National Educational Technology Standards (NETS) and are designed for beginner, intermediate, or advanced levels, aimed at middle school and secondary students.http://www.microsoft.com/education/teachers/guides/critical_thinking.aspx?WT.mc_id=criticalthinking_redu_site

Betsy Moore & Todd Stanley: Critical Thinking and Formative Assessments: Increasing Rigor in Your Classroom. Building from a careful explanation of Bloom's Taxonomy, this 2010 title provides many practical classroom applications to help teachers promote critical thinking in a variety of subject areas. Strategies that can be immediately put to use in the classroom are found throughout.

David N. Perkins, Heidi Goodrich, Shari Tishman, & Jill Mirman Owen: *Thinking Connections: Learning to Think and Thinking to Learn*. This title from Harvard's Project Zero research group includes step-by-step instructions and practical suggestions for teaching three critical thinking strategies. http://pzpublications.com/31.html

Peter Senge: The Fifth Discipline and **The Fifth Discipline Fieldbook.** These two titles were among the first—and are still among the best—introductions to system thinking for educators and other professional who want to make their workplaces into 21st century learning organizations.

Linda Booth Sweeney: The Systems Thinking Playbook. This title, aimed at K–12 teachers, university faculty, and organizational consultants, provides 30 short gaming exercises, classified by areas of learning—Mental Models, Team Learning, Systems

Thinking, Shared Vision, and Personal Mastery. The companion DVD shows good practices for introducing and conducting the games. To purchase the Playbook, contact linda@lindaboothsweeney.net.

GENERAL PD RESOURCES

The Center for Creative Learning, based in Sarasota, FL, offers a variety of publications, training programs, information support, and consulting services on creativity, creative problem solving, talent development, and learning styles. http://www.creativelearning.com/

The Waters Foundation: Systems Thinking in Schools. The Water Foundation website offers classroom lessons, research, and best practices, as well as information on their workshops and online learning materials—all on educational applications of systems thinking. http://www.watersfoundation.org/

The Creative Learning Exchange focuses its efforts on K–12 educators to help them teach systems thinking and system dynamics to enable students the interconnected challenges that face them at personal, community, and global levels. Their website features a library of free downloaded resources, as well as the opportunity to learn more about their conferences, newsletter, and listserve.http://www.clexchange.org/

CLASSROOM RESOURCES: These resources are designed for classroom use to promote students' collaboration skills

RUBRICS

Catalina Foot Hills Critical Thinking Rubric. Catalina Foothills School District created a series of rubrics to assess student critical thinking skills. The rubric measures critical thinking skills such as comparing, classifying, inductive and deductive reasoning, error analysis, and decision making.
http://www.p21.org/route21/index.php?option=com_jlibrary&view=details&id=160

First Lego League Rubrics. Rubrics for the FIRST LEGO League (FLL) robotics program not only focus on STEM but also stress teamwork and collaboration, communication skills, creativity and innovation, and critical thinking. http://www.p21.org/route21/index.php?option=com_jlibrary&view=details&id=939.

Additional resources are available at Route 21, visit www.p21.org/route21 And at www.p21.org, select Skills Maps and find classroom resources in Arts, Geography, Science, Social Studies, and English.

Professional Development Resources
Creativity and Innovation

Think Creatively
- Use a wide range of idea creation techniques (such as brainstorming)
- Create new and worthwhile ideas (both incremental and radical concepts)
- Elaborate, refine, analyze, and evaluate their own ideas in order to improve and maximize creative efforts

Work Creatively with Others
- Develop, implement, and communicate new ideas to others effectively
- Be open and responsive to new and diverse perspectives; incorporate group input and feedback into the work
- Demonstrate originality and inventiveness in work and understand the real-world limits to adopting new ideas
- View failure as an opportunity to learn; understand that creativity and innovation is a long-term, cyclical process of small successes and frequent mistakes

Implement Innovations
- Act on creative ideas to make a tangible and useful contribution to the field in which the innovation will occur

---

PROFESSIONAL DEVELOPMENT: The following resources help teachers understand how to promote the creativity and innovation skills of their students.

PROFESSIONAL DEVELOPMENT VIDEO with accompanying PD TOOLS
ASCD: *Promoting Creativity and Innovation in the Classroom*. Drawing from what innovative Fortune 500 companies do to promote creativity and innovation in the workplace, this video shows real-world strategies for classroom curricula and instruction.
 http://shop.ascd.org/productdisplay.cfm?categoryid=books&productid=609096

ONLINE PD COURSE
CyberSmart: *Authentic Learning and Creativity*. This workshop provide educators with hands-on practice in engaging students real-world tasks that require the use of technology, and in exploring ways of developing students' creative thinking.
http://cybersmart.org/workshops/smart/learningcreativity/

PD BOOKS

Project Zero, a research center located at Harvard Graduate School of Education, publishes a number of titles on creativity, with a special focus on how teachers can promote it in their classrooms. For a listing, see http://pzpublications.com/creativity.html

Meg Ormiston: *Creating a Digitally Rich Classroom: Teaching and Learning in a Web 2.0 World*. This book provides a research base and practical strategies for using Web 2.0 tools to create engaging lessons that transform and enrich content. For more information, visit http://www.solution-tree.com/Public/Media.aspx?ShowDetail=true&ProductID=BKF385

Daniel Pink: *A Whole New Mind Why Right-Brainers Will Rule the Future.* This book reveals the six essential aptitudes on which professional success and personal fulfillment now depend, and includes a series of hands-on exercises culled from experts around the world to help readers sharpen the necessary abilities. This book will change not only how we see the world but how we experience it as well.

Richard Florida: *The Flight of the Creative Class.* This book focuses on economic growth and the fact that the key lies not just in the ability to attract the creative class, but to translate that underlying advantage into creative economic outcomes in the form of new ideas, new high-tech businesses, and regional growth.

Ken Robinson: *Out of Our Minds: Learning to be Creative*. This book was described by *Director* magazine as "a truly mind opening analysis of why we don't get the best out of people at a time of punishing change."

PD ARTICLES

Paul Torrance: *Creativity in the Classroom—What Research Says to the Teacher.* This booklet discusses this creativity and explores the evidences of change in educational objectives, teaching methods, curriculum and instructional materials, procedures for identifying creative talent, and the assessment of creative achievement. For a link to the full article, see http://eric.ed.gov/ERICWebPortal/search/detailmini.jsp?_nfpb=true&_&ERICExtSearch_SearchValue_0=ED132593&ERICExtSearch_SearchType_0=no&accno=ED132593

Alice Sterling Honig: *Professional Development: Supporting Creativity in the Classroom.* This article underscores the importance of creative thinking in your educational program, especially in getting children to think "outside the box." For a link to the full article, see http://www2.scholastic.com/browse/article.jsp?id=10583

CLASSROOM RESOURCES: These resources are designed for classroom use to promote students' creativity and innovation skills.

GENERAL CREATIVITY EXAMPLES
The Kennedy Center: *ArtsEdge*. This rich website features lessons, activities, projects, and curriculum guidelines for educators to use to promote creativity in the arts, history, literature, and other humanities disciplines. In addition, there are a wealth of multimedia resources and ideas for encouraging the use of technology as a creative educational tool. http://artsedge.kennedy-center.org/educators.aspx

Intel: *Visual Ranking, Seeing Reason,* **and** *Showing Evidence Tools*. These free online tools are effective ways of bringing idea creation techniques into the classroom. Tutorials, project examples, and instructional strategies are also provided. http://www.intel.com/education/teachers/

IDEO. http://www.ideo.com/ The world-renowned design firm, Ideo's website provides creative ideas on how we will do routine tasks in the future. The site also provides a wealth of resources on design thinking, "… a human-centered approach to innovation" that marries design methodology with technology and knowledge of how humans interact with the world.

Additional resources are available at Route 21, visit www.p21.org/route21
And at www.p21.org , select Skills Maps and find classroom resources in Arts, Geography, Science, Social Studies, and English.

Professional Development Resources
Communication

Communicate Clearly
- Articulate thoughts and ideas effectively using oral, written, and nonverbal communication skills in a variety of forms and contexts
- Listen effectively to decipher meaning, including knowledge, values, attitudes, and intentions
- Use communication for a range of purposes (e.g., to inform, instruct, motivate, and persuade)
- Utilize multiple media and technologies, and know how to judge their effectiveness a priori as well as assess their impact
- Communicate effectively in diverse environments (including multilingual)

PROFESSIONAL DEVELOPMENT: The following professional development resources help teachers understand how to promote the 21st century communication skills of their students.

ONLINE RESOURCES

The Center for Media Literacy's website offers a rich array of tools and best practices for helping teachers develop their students' media literacy skills. In addition to its highly regarded Media Literacy Toolkit, the center also offers professional development services directly to schools.
http://www.medialit.org/professional-development

Edutopia: Tech Integration. This portion of the George Lucas Foundation's Edutopia website offers a wealth of videos, articles, and best practice case studies on the use of technology as an essential communication tool in 21st century learning environments. Also included are community resources such as blogs and discussion forums, as well as real-world examples, and profiles of schools and educators who are leading the way in ICT literacy. http://www.edutopia.org/tech-integration

TEACHER STANDARDS
ISTE: NETS for Teachers 2008. Widely adopted and recognized, the NETS integrate

educational technology standards for educators involved with any educational curricula, and can be used for technology planning and curriculum development at both primary and secondary school levels. The NETS for Teachers focuses on the skills and knowledge educators need to teach, work, and learn in an increasingly connected global and digital society.
http://www.iste.org/standards/nets-for-teachers/nets-for-teachers-2008.aspx

ARTICLES

Education Leadership Journal: *Literacy 2.0.* The March 2009 issue of this leading professional publication contains a number of useful articles on the topic of literacy in the 21st century. Collectively, this issue addresses the questions: what does literacy mean in the 21st century, and how do we as educators help our students effective manage, analyze, and create information today?

BOOKS

Richard Murnane & Frank Levy: Teaching the New Basic Skills and **The New Division of Labor.** These books make the case for complex communication and expert thinking skills as essential components of every student's education. Murnane and Levy, economists at Harvard and MIT respectively, argue persuasively that these skills, once the domain of the elite, must be widely mastered to ensure, not just individual success, but also our nation's economic health.

CLASSROOM RESOURCES: These resources are designed for classroom use to promote students' collaboration skills.

RUBRICS

Lawrence Township Interactive Communication Rubric. Lawrence Township created a rubric to assess interactive communication in the following areas: digital environments, media, range of expression, mode of interaction, management, communities of interest, personal interaction, and ethics.
http://www.p21.org/route21/index.php?option=com_jlibrary&view=details&id=323

21st Century Communication Rubric. Rio Vista Elementary uses this rubric to measure students' communications skills. It offers strategies for clearly evaluating oral and written communications, as well as the usage of presentation tools and technology.
http://www.p21.org/route21/index.php?option=com_jlibrary&view=details&id=849

STUDENT STANDARDS

American Association of School Librarians: *Information Literacy Standards for Students.*
These comprehensive standards provide a conceptual framework and broad guidelines for

describing the information-literate student. http://www.ala.org/ala/mgrps/divs/aasl/
aaslarchive/pubsarchive/informationpower/InformationLiteracyStandards_final.pdf

ISTE: NETS for Students
Widely adopted and recognized, the NETS for Students integrate educational technology
standards across all educational curricula and at all student levels. While most educational
standards apply to a specific content area, the NETS are not subject-matter specific, but
rather a compendium of skills required for students to be competitive and successful in a
global and digital world.
http://www.iste.org/standards/nets-for-students/nets-student-standards-2007.aspx

ASSESSMENTS
iCriticalThinking: This outcomes-based assessment, developed by ETS and Certiport,
assesses the ability of students to think critically and solve real-world problems using a
range of information and communication technology (ICT) literacy skills. For more
information, see http://www.ets.org/icriticalthinking/about

Additional resources are available at Route 21, visit www.p21.org/route21
And at www.p21.org , select Skills Maps and find classroom resources in Arts, Geography,
Science, Social Studies, and English.

Professional Development Resources
Collaboration

Collaborate with Others
- Demonstrate ability to work effectively and respectfully with diverse teams
- Exercise flexibility and willingness to be helpful in making necessary compromises to accomplish a common goal
- Assume shared responsibility for collaborative work, and value the individual contributions made by each team member

---

PROFESSIONAL DEVELOPMENT: The following professional development resources help teachers understand how to promote the collaboration skills of their students.

ONLINE PD COURSES

Intel Education: *Collaboration in the Digital Classroom.* Intel offers free just-in-time online professional development to enable teachers to explore 21st century learning concepts. Facilitation materials are also available free of charge. Intel's collaboration course helps teachers develop activities that prepare students to collaborate in the digital global world of the 21st century.
http://www.intel.com/education/video/collaborate/content.htm (also available on CD)

Marilyn Gootman: *Classroom Management: Building Effective Relationships.* In this ASCD course, the focus is on helping teachers promote cooperation and collaboration with and among students in their classrooms.
http://shop.ascd.org/productdisplay.cfm?productid=PD09OC02

PD VIDEO

ITC Publications: *The TeacherPD Video series*. This Australian company offers training video vodcasts and dozens of writable templates that feature their classroom-based collaborative learning tools. http://www.itcpublications.com.au/

BOOK

Project Zero: *Making Teaching Visible.* From Harvard's Project Zero research group, this title presents research on individual and group learning contexts and provides professional development supports for teachers. http://www.pzpublications.com/133.html

E-BOOK
Douglas Fischer & Nancy Frey. *Better Learning Through Structured Teaching: A Framework for the Gradual Release of Responsibility.* This ASCD publication helps teachers develop effective strategies for promoting independent, small-group, and collaborative learning. http://shop.ascd.org/productdisplay.cfm?productid=108010E4

CLASSROOM RESOURCES: These resources are designed for classroom use to promote students' collaboration skills.

RUBRICS
SDSU: *Collaboration Rubric.* Developed by a group of California scientists as part of a fourth grade project in which students investigate tidal pools, this rubric functions independently of the content area. It is appropriate for elementary school collaborative work, and could easily be adapted to middle and high school use. http://edweb.sdsu.edu/triton/tidepoolunit/Rubrics/collrubric.html

Additional resources are available at Route 21, visit www.p21.org/route21
And at www.p21.org , select Skills Maps and find classroom resources in Arts, Geography, Science, Social Studies, and English.

Index